PANDORA PRESS

RUNNING

Liz Sloan was born in 1947. She began running when she was twenty-nine, has taken part in two London Marathons, and has run for Sussex County. In 1982 she organised the first UK Women's Day of Sport. As a result of that event and of her experience as a runner, she firmly believes that running is a means to liberation for women. Liz teaches full-time, lectures on women and sport, and is married with two children.

Ann Kramer was born in 1946. She has worked in publishing since 1970 as an editor and freelance writer. She has written on various aspects of women and health and was the editor of *Woman's Body: An Owner's Manual* (Paddington Press, 1977), as well as contributing to various other publications. She is a committed feminist, has a young daughter, and is currently studying for a History B.A. at Sussex University.

PANDORA HANDBOOK

Your Body, Your Baby, Your Life

A non-patronising, non-moralising, non-sexist guide to pregnancy and childbirth

Angela Phillips
with Nicky Lean & Barbara Jacob
Illustrated by Ros Asquith

Discovering Women's History

A practical manual

Deirdre Beddoe

Autumn 1985

On Your Own

A practical guide to independent living

Jean Shapiro

Getting Jobs in Film and Television

A Woman's Handbook

Ann Ross-Muir in association with Sandra Horne, Equality Officer, ACTT

This list is continually growing to meet the changing needs of women in the 1980's. We welcome proposals and enquiries from our readership.

RUNNING
THE WOMEN'S HANDBOOK

LIZ SLOAN & ANN KRAMER

Illustrated by Elaine Anderson
with Cartoons by Jo Nesbitt

ANDORA PRESS

London, Boston, Melbourne and Henley

First published in 1985
by (Routledge & Kegan Paul plc) Pandora Press

14 Leicester Square, London WC2H 7PH, England

9 Park Street, Boston, Mass. 02108, USA

464 St Kilda Road, Melbourne,
Victoria 3004, Australia and

Broadway House, Newtown Road,
Henley on Thames, Oxon RG9 1EN, England

Set in 9 on 11 point Melior
by Columns of Reading
and printed in Great Britain
by Cox and Wyman Ltd,
Reading, Berks.

Library of Congress Cataloging in Publication Data
Sloan, Liz, 1947-
Running, the women's handbook.
(Pandora handbook)
Bibliography: p.
Includes index.
1. Running for women. I. Kramer, Ann,
1946-   . II. Title.
GV1061.18.W66S56   1985   796.4′26   85-536

British Library CIP data also available

ISBN 0-86358-043-2

CONTENTS

Foreword vii
Chris Benning

Acknowledgments ix

Introduction xi
Liz Sloan

1 **Women talk about running** 1
Claudia: 'if you can run, we can clap' (p. 1); Mary: 'fag in
one hand, whisky in the other' (p. 3); Chris: 'unfit,
unhealthy and unhappy' (p. 4)

2 **Why running?** 8
Fitness – a general feeling of well-being (p. 8); Causes of
unfitness (p. 9); So – why running? (p. 13)

3 **Women with disabilities** 15
Sport doesn't come easily (p. 19); Medical classification for
athletes with disabilities (p. 19); An athlete in her own
right (p. 20); It's not all downhill (p. 21); Problems (p. 23)

4 **Running through time** 25
Men only (p. 25); Government warning: sport can damage
your health (p. 26); Bicycles and bloomers (p. 28); You
can't be an athlete and a woman too (p. 29); You can play
but you can't compete (p. 30); Into the eighties (p. 33)

5 **Running on the spot: how it is today** 36
Nice legs, shame about the face (p. 39); Female or not?
(p. 40); Recent developments (p. 43)

6 **The barriers in front of women** 46
But I don't know how to run (p. 46); But it's so masculine
(p. 47); But everyone will see me (p. 50); But I haven't got
the time (p. 52); So why the barriers? (p. 53)

7 **The weaker sex? Exploding the myths** 55
Sport is counter-reproductive: you can't be a mother and

an athlete too (p. 55); Anything we can do, they can do better – or can they? (p. 59); But can you be an athlete and a woman too? (p. 63)

8 **Getting started**   **65**
You can lead a horse to water but you can't make it drink (p. 65); Think positive – it's all in the mind – or is it? (p. 65); Before you start: safety checks (p. 69); Starting off (p. 70); Just relax (p. 71); Where to run (p. 72); All kinds of weather (p. 73); What to wear (p. 74); Shoes (p. 75); Clothes (p. 76); What not to wear (p. 78); Organising your day (p. 79); Beginner's schedule (p. 80); Minor problems (p. 83); Helpful ideas (p. 85); Diet (p. 87)

9 **Keep on running**   **89**
The human machine: running and your body (p. 89); Checking your pulse (p. 92); What next? Keeping going (p. 92); Making choices (p. 93); Putting up your distance – getting a 'bigger dose' (p. 93); Thinking about racing – you don't have to be good (p. 94); Being prepared: the need for training (p. 96); Training (p. 97); Types of races (p. 101); Equipment (p. 104); The need for care (p. 104); Prevention is better than cure (p. 105); Warming up and warming down (p. 105); Mobilising exercises (p. 106); Stretching exercises (p. 106); Injuries (p. 107); Training schedules (p. 112)

10 **Women helping women**   **118**
A first for women: the Hastings Women's Day of Sport (p. 118); Starting a running club (p. 123)

11 **Where to next? Mobilising ourselves**   **124**

Useful addresses   **128**

Further reading   **133**

Index   **136**

FOREWORD

If Liz Sloan had nine lives she would still find she did not have enough time to pursue all her interests. In addition to working full-time, looking after two children, running, supporting the Campaign for Nuclear Disarmament, vegetarian cookery and giving lectures on women and sport, she has found time to write this book – an amazing feat!

Unlike Liz, who did not begin running until she was twenty-nine, I have been running since I was a toddler. My parents had both enjoyed athletics, and I have an uncle and cousin who competed at county level. All of them were delighted when I joined my local athletics club at the age of twelve, stimulated by finishing fourth in the Town Sports over 60 yards. Sprinting, however, took a back seat once I tried 880 yards and actually won my first race over that distance. I gained my first senior international vest in 1974, and won the English National Cross Country Championships the following year. In 1978 I won a silver medal in the Commonwealth Games. The following season I broke the UK record twice and devoted my entire time to training. For various reasons this turned out to be a mistake, and I sustained a few injuries as well as a mineral imbalance.

I was delighted to qualify for the 1984 Olympics and enjoyed the experience so much that I have vowed to try and make it to the 1988 Olympics to be held in Seoul. Nowadays there is a precedent for carrying on with one's sport and there appears to be no reason to give up. Certainly, like Liz, I have made running an integral part of my life.

In fact Liz and I share many interests, our love of running obviously, but also our deep concern to encourage more women to share this passion. Liz and I met at a 10-mile road race where we (and our husbands) were competing. I can't remember how we fared but the women's prizes were half the value of the men's. Such discrimination is hardly encouraging and is a regular occurrence in our sport at a competitive level.

Times are changing slowly and Liz and I like to think we have contributed to the growing number of women taking up running today, Liz by her First Women's Day of Sport, and my Women and Running Seminar held in March 1984. The latter attracted 141 women who came to listen to lectures on medical aspects of running, injuries, training and 'a liberated view of running' presented by Dr Lynn Fitzgerald. Lynn highlighted some of the problems for women when she described the Battersea multigym which is situated in the men's changing room, hardly encouraging women to share the facilities! Certainly the day fulfilled my hopes that women with a similar interest would get together, learn about their sport, and share their experiences and I hope this book will go much further in spreading the word.

Women are slowly emerging from the confines of socially acceptable female sports such as tennis and keep fit. The media hinders this move with its constant reference to the age and appearance of the 'girls'. Perhaps this book will help to re-educate some of the commentators and reporters in the sport.

Finally, I'd like to add how much I admire Liz for writing this book; it has taken me at least five months to write this foreword. Good luck Liz.

Chris Benning

ACKNOWLEDGMENTS

Firstly we would like to thank our children – Sarah, Tom and Matthew – for their extraordinary patience. For them the last six months have been marked by considerable neglect, punctuated only by irritable cries of 'No, I can't I'm working on the book'. We are very grateful to them for their love and co-operation.

Also we want to thank the many women who gave us so much of their time by allowing us to interview and to talk to them about running, and many of whose experiences and thoughts appear in this book. Our thanks to Claudia, Chris, Kathleen, Mary, Eileen, Val, Cecily, Kim, Denise, Karen and the many women who filled in our questionnaires. We hope that this book expresses their views as well as our own.

In addition we would like to thank Jackie Warrington and Jim Atkinson of the Sports Council, Malcolm Clark, Simon Lynn of the BSAD, the Consumer's Association for permission to reprint material from the June 1984 issue of Which? and also the many people who have sent us information no matter how small. A special thanks to Simon Adams for his encouragement and advice right at the time when we were still wondering whether there was a book to write or not. Finally authors traditionally, and rightly, thank their typists and we would like to thank Bob Sloan who not only lived cheerfully with this book for the last six months but also equally cheerfully typed many of the chapters. We would like to thank Philippa Brewster and Pandora for their support.

Finally we would like to thank our many friends in Hastings and outside who have been so supportive during the writing of this book.

INTRODUCTION

I never thought I would ever write a book. But here it is. Ann has, and she's worked as an editor on many books. She never thought that she would even consider jogging. But she has.

Ann's house is full of bookshelves, filled with rows of books packed tight, ordered and neat. Our house is piled high with boxes of running shoes spilling out all over the place and is a shambles.

I can't remember when I met Ann or even how; it might have been through a local women's group we were both in during the 1970s. Yet it is only in the last two years that we have become good friends. It was after Shiona and I did the Women's Day of Sport in 1982 (see page 118), that we made contact again. I discussed doing a booklet about the day, so there and then Ann helped me to work out a format. After we had done it, I said 'You know Ann, there are no running books in the UK written by women for women'. So, at the end of the format for the Women's Day booklet, Ann typed: Next project – women's running book. It was Ann who got me knuckled down; I was always too busy running or teaching. Ann also gave me the confidence to do it, without her it would never have got done.

I started running when I was twenty-nine, and a roll-your-own smoker. Bob, my husband, was already running. On cold winter nights I would be huddled in our front room, cold and smoking. Bob would come in from a run sweating, hot and fanning the air with his hand, and complain about the heat in the house and the smell of tobacco.

A fun game of football during that Easter holidays put me off smoking. Then Bob suggested that I started running. No was my answer at first. I did a few 100m sprints at a track meeting, and found that I couldn't do it. I also tried to run half a mile, and found that that was impossible. At the time I had planned a visit to Norway with my youngest son, where we were going to work in a youth hostel in the mountains. A keen American runner was also staying there plus another American who wanted to start running, so we started together, and ran to a bridge and back. When I arrived home again I was a bit fitter. Bob persuaded me to run in a cross country race (which was an annual event) in a month's time. So I had one month to work up to 2 miles. Well I did it and ran the race. I felt great afterwards and that was it. I was totally addicted; three years later, in fact, I finally won that race. There were no other women for me to run with at the time, and I found it hard training with men, and also training on the track. But it certainly acted as a stimulus when one particular man used to stand watching, telling me not to join in training sessions with the men. Of course I carried on and my enthusiasm increased even more when I beat Bob's time in my fourth 1500m race.

I believed then, and I do now, that women are strong and that age doesn't matter. Women seem to get stronger as they mature; the main requisite is to believe in ourselves. Running has become very much a part of our life as a family, and an essential part of my life as an individual woman. It is my freedom, my time to myself. And it is this we have tried to express in the book, and just how important running is for women.

The fact that Ann hadn't done anything to keep fit before the book was important: it meant that she had plenty of questions so we hope that her questions as a new jogger match the questions that most other women might ask. We also hope the book is enjoyable, and that there might be a few laughs and not too many tears.

We appreciate enormously the support that world-class athletes such as Chris Benning have given to women and to this book. And also international athletes such as Caroline Rodgers who has known for years that women runners are trivialised and not accepted on equal terms with men. We hope this book expresses their beliefs and aspirations as well as our own.

Finally, Ann and I both believe that running is another and very crucial way for women to control their own bodies and their own lives. It sometimes wasn't easy to write this book because we got angry at just how many barriers there are in front of women, just how often women are put down. But it's because Ann and I share deeply the belief in women's own potential that we were, with our different but complementary skills, able to work together to produce this book. We hope you enjoy it, and that it will encourage you to run.

Liz Sloan

1 WOMEN TALK ABOUT RUNNING

Claudia: 'if you can run, we can clap'

Claudia is American. She is forty-five years old and started running when she was thirty-eight. As she describes it: 'I love running, it is an addiction. It's a pleasant, sensual feeling of being in the air, of being more in the air than on the ground, as though I am a passenger being carried in my own body'.

Claudia started running as a result of watching the 1977 New York Marathon in which her husband was taking part. She says 'It was so much fun. It was big, exciting and marvellous'. As she stood there among the crowds of spectators, having seen her husband run by, she watched some of the runners slow down to a walk. Suddenly she felt an overwhelming urge to run when the crowd began to clap the tired runners shouting 'If you can run, we can clap'. For Claudia that was it. After watching that event, she herself began to run and only four months later actually entered and completed her first marathon.

As Claudia says, 'It was extraordinary. I didn't do any sport at school. I couldn't even play soft ball, my hand-eye co-ordination was so appallingly awful.' As a girl she remembers being kept in the gym after school practising basketball until she could do a 'put-up shot' – running by the basket and dropping the ball in. Apparently she ran by the basket so many times without success that her exasperated teacher finally released her because she had to go home. For Claudia the experience was so humiliating that she would 'rather have crawled over broken glass'. Little wonder then that Claudia chose brains and academic achievement in preference to sport. Today one of the things that Claudia most resents about those school days is that she saw herself as untalented and as a result missed out on running. 'Why didn't somebody give me a chance; why didn't somebody tell me?' For when Claudia did run she found that in fact she had a lot of stamina and some speed.

When Claudia started running she was living in the United States with her English husband, Ron. Their lives were very busy. Claudia was doing research for an anthropological study of the area, Ron worked full-time, and they had three children aged between one and ten years old. Despite these commitments, Claudia set aside time for running whenever she could, convinced that the energy she gave to running was a very real investment, and she could spare it. She even remembers jogging with her daughter Hazel on her back in order to make time for her run. As she says,

> 'Even on the days that you decide you won't run, that you are too tired, and that the weather's rotten or that you have too much to do, you find yourself looking out of the window, thinking well I'll just go for a little run. And it is always worth it. Doing that run gives you such a sense of well-being, really it is doing something that your body is designed to do. Running is the biggest discovery I made, and the most important.'

For Claudia running has also meant new friends and real comradeship. Interestingly, she also says that in no other field has she met so little male chauvinism and so much companionship as among runners. Female and male runners alike, she says, take a real interest in each other's achievements, asking about their race times, checking on health, sharing a common denomenator: running. As time passes, too, the same faces turn up each year at the same events so that bonds and friendships are formed. It can and does work the other way, and there's no doubt that some male runners feel threatened by women runners. Claudia remembers when she was running in the US Marine Half-Marathon, and passing one male marine after another, all of them identical with crew cuts and T-shirts emblazoned with 'Stripped for Action and Action Ready' printed on them. As she says, 'They all looked so similar I began to think I was passing the same man each time. And they weren't very pleased to be passed by a woman. In fact, if you want to see dismay made flesh, be a woman and run past a marine.'

Today Claudia lives in England. And she's still running. But she does find a difference between the two countries. When she started running in the small American town where she lived, everybody else seemed to be running too and there was a great deal of interest and enthusiasm. Here, she says, far fewer women run. And what she finds is that 'women look at me running and say "I should be doing what you are doing" '. In response Claudia feels that she wants to stop and say:

'No, it isn't that you *should* be running, you have enough things in your life that you *should* be doing – like working, seeing your husband's family, shopping or cleaning the house . . . . Running is the means of escaping all that. It shouldn't become yet another source of guilt.'

Mary: 'fag in one hand, whisky in the other'

Mary started running on her fifty-ninth birthday. Just like Claudia she was also watching a marathon: the London Marathon. But, unlike Claudia, Mary was watching it at home on the television. Even so the atmosphere seemed to come straight through the screen because sitting there 'fag in one hand, whisky in the other', Mary suddenly thought 'I can do that'.

Through the British Sunday *Observer* newspaper, the marathon organisers were asking for volunteer runners so Mary applied, was accepted, and was sent a training programme. Mary's decision coincided with her retirement which had left her on a reduced income of £40 a week. For financial reasons alone, cigarettes could no longer take priority on the shopping list, and the marathon provided a second good reason to stop smoking. She did, and apart from improving her health, also began to save £1 a week.

For Mary, like so many other women, running was a completely new departure. She had done no sport since she was sixteen years old, although she had always been active and had enjoyed walking. She found, however, that running held more surprises than she had imagined. The first time Mary went out she decided to run until she was absolutely exhausted and to time herself in order to check how long she had run for. As Mary says, 'I charged off, hurtled along the park at great speed, stopped and crashed against a tree, completely shattered'. When she looked at her watch, Mary found she had only been running for 2 minutes!

After this experience Mary built up her running rather more slowly. She decided to do her training early in the morning. On one of her first runs she put on her shorts, and made her way out of the front door blithely assuming that as it was 6am on a Saturday morning nobody would be about. However, she saw someone she knew on the other side of the road. Immediately she went back in and closed the door! Mary's next thought was 'how silly' and out she went again. Her neighbour asked where Mary was going, and Mary replied 'running', a statement that she thought was unnecessary as she was wearing shorts after all. As Mary remarks 'My friends thought I was quite mad'!

Mary enjoyed running. She remembers in particular one very early morning run that she did with a friend, running through the woods where she found an injured bird. She loved the feeling at the end of a run, as she came round the corner to home, looking forward to a hot shower, and proud in the knowledge that she had just run 10 miles.

Mary continued her training right up to the day of the London Marathon. When she arrived in Greenwich Park, she found it both exciting and amusing to see the park full of people stretching and limbering up. A strange smell was wafting around and Mary noticed to her amusement, that people were rubbing linament into their legs and vaseline into their feet.

Mary ran the London Marathon in 5 hours 4 minutes although she insists on taking 7 minutes off that time as it took her that long to get from Greenwich Park to the official start line. She enjoyed the Marathon enormously and found it a marvellous experience. Unfortunately she strained her knee and has not run since but is being encouraged to start again by other women runners. Apparently Mary is now considering the New York Marathon. She has decided to run with a whisky in one hand but doesn't know what to carry in the other.

Chris: 'unfit, unhealthy and unhappy'

Chris is thirty and started running when she was twenty-eight. At the time she says she was 'unfit, unhealthy, and unhappy. I was aware of the fact that I was fast approaching thirty, and could easily slip into "unhealthy" middle age unless I started regular exercise.'

Chris also had problems in her marriage, was unemployed and was looking for something that would give her the independence of mind and body that she felt she needed. 'I smoked heavily, felt tired and lethargic most of the time, but more than anything lacked confidence in myself. Quite frankly, living had become a struggle and I knew that I had to take control or do something with myself.'

A chat with a friend produced that 'something'. A Woman's Day of Sport at the local sports centre had inspired her friend to take up jogging, so Chris decided to have a go as well.

'I already had a pair of trainers – they were the fashionable footwear of the time – and I borrowed a T-shirt and shorts from my friend. I felt an incredible determination to give up smoking and to really work at getting fit. I also needed a channel for my frustration from my marriage. I know it sounds dramatic to say "that first run changed my life" but time has shown that since then my life has gone in a completely new direction.'

Like many women, Chris's low self-esteem made her underestimate her abilities. But running 2 miles at her first attempt was all she needed to make her realize that running was an activity worth pursuing. She had, in fact, tried to run about a year before with her husband but

'after about half a mile I was exhausted because he went too fast. There always was this business of competition between us – once again I was led by a man into an activity which he was fairly good at. I, as the woman, was always behind, so I gave up running after that because if I was to do anything, I wanted it to be mine and not directed or controlled by my husband. This second time the people I ran with encouraged and helped me without the competition and threat I'd felt from him.'

However, Chris made the mistake of pushing herself too far too soon. This can be a problem with keen new runners who set themselves unrealistic goals and so injure themselves. And after her first six months, having started racing as well as running for fun, Chris was exhausted.

'When I'm injured, I notice a depressing, vicious circle of events – I start smoking but the more I smoke the more I lose confidence in my ability to run, so I don't run and I smoke even more. It's certainly a problem for me, as is weight control, but being so much more aware of myself it makes me face these problems head on. I now try and combine running with swimming and cycling so that I keep fit but don't overdo it. I *need* the "drug" of exercise. During that difficult time when my marriage was breaking up, running helped me cope with tremendous strain and hassles. I didn't need calming drugs even though I felt tense and threatened. I just went on my daily run to help me through.'

What Chris gains from running is what many women gain. But there is no magic formula. To continue running does involve self-discipline, something that women are not very good at when it comes to making a commitment to do something just for themselves. As Chris says:

'Me, making time for *my* running, has made me realise just how much we parcel out our time according to what others, particularly a man if we are with one, want us to do. So it's good to have the willpower to do such a personal, private activity.'

Running plays a very important part in Chris's life as a single woman. After her marriage ended, she found it easy to lose confidence in herself as a woman, and to doubt her inner strength. Being on her own, she has a lot of decisions to make about her job, home and so on – sometimes quite mundane matters but not always so – and running has definitely given her confidence to deal with these and helped her to cope with this single, 'alone' status, not easy to do when you have shared your life with someone else for nine years. Perhaps she best sums it up in her own words:

'Now that I do run regularly, I notice that I have much more energy and generally feel alive. I hate having to stay indoors and love being outside – something that never concerned me before. Being fit, healthy and feeling muscles develop is also important. The feeling of well-being becomes a way of life. I notice that I'm far less tolerant of things that really do annoy me because I have much more confidence in my needs and desires. Yet, at the same time, I feel really happy after a run, calm inside and much more able to cope with my problems and the stresses of everyday life and relationships. I always have the same feeling after a good run: that I'm strong and o.k., that I can cope with anything and I'll be alright no matter what happens. I think that women lack this confidence on the whole, and tend to rely on more superficial things such as their appearance to boost their self-esteem. The great thing about running is that your physical self improves anyway; what is more important is that you gain inner strength and confidence.

I used to be sluggish, lazy and physically inactive, but now it's the opposite. I need activity and most of the time I actually like myself. I enjoy using my body. Hopefully by the time I'm forty I'll be fitter than ever before in my life – that's what I'd like to aim at.'

2 *WHY RUNNING?*

'I sleep longer and sounder. I find I am more alert during the day. It's my running and I like it; it makes me feel special.'

(Julia, a woman runner)

If someone came to you with a pill and said that it would give you health, mental and physical fitness, better concentration, the ability to cope with stress and work, greater self-esteem, new friends and companionship, self-awareness and a whole way of life, you would take it. But there is no such pill. Instead all these are things that women runners say running has given them.

As women we are burdened with anxieties about our appearance. Magazines, newspaper articles and television constantly bombard us with the images of 'ideal' womanhood – lithe, beautiful and desirable – so much so that there is hardly a woman who doesn't feel insecure about some part of her body or even all of it. And there's no doubt that, today, anything to do with sport for women sells itself on just that image.

Running, like a lot of other sports, does add sparkle to your eyes, firms up your breasts, and keeps you trim. But for women running goes much deeper. It alters your life, gives you health and confidence, and ultimately changes the very way you think about yourself. And running gives us time to ourselves. Confidence and time – two things that women rarely have. Our traditional role as women demands that we be sensitive to the needs of others – lovers, husbands and children – to put their wishes before our own. We make time for others but rarely take it for ourselves.

Today, women of all ages are putting on their track suits in all weathers and are taking to the roads, parks and streets. Many of them have never taken an interest in sport before; many have found time they never thought they had. All of them are discovering benefits they would never have imagined.

Fitness – a general feeling of well-being

'Fitness, freedom, enjoyment and a sense of achievement' – that's how one woman describes what she gets from running. Many other women runners feel the same way including Chris, Claudia and myself. 'Fitness', however, is a term we use a lot but many of us don't really know what we mean by it. During our research for part of this book, Ann and I went round the local schools asking young people about sport. One of the questions we asked was why they thought that sport was on the school curriculum. 'Well, it keeps you fit', some replied. But asked if they knew what fitness was, they weren't too sure. Nor, interestingly, were most of them taught the benefits of sport.

I am sure that before most of us started running, or even thought of running, we would have described ourselves as being at least as fit as most other people. But it is an illusion, and until you put your body to the test, there is no way of knowing just how fit or unfit you are. Through running, however, not only does the body become fitter, but the runner herself becomes more body conscious, more in tune with the condition of, and changes to, her body. She can actually make a comparison between her before and after self, between her fit and unfit self.

In fact I can date exactly when I knew that I was unfit. In 1976 when I was twenty-nine I played a game of football with some other women. Previous to that game, I had thought of myself as young and reasonably fit, despite the fact that I smoked. I spent most of the game running up and down the pitch, and afterwards my lungs were tight, I could taste blood and, for the first time, realised just how out of condition I was. Shortly afterwards I started running. I can certainly now play a game of football for an hour or more without any ill effects.

So what exactly is fitness? It is a term that is notoriously hard to define. It's a relative concept, affected by health, age, body type, gender and so on. Even so, fitness might best be described as the ability to perform tasks with the minimum of effort. Essentially it is getting the very best possible use out of your body, something that few women are encouraged to do. Fitness is associated with efficiency; the fitter you are, the more efficiently your body is working, and in particular the heart and lungs, and not only your body – fitness affects us both physically and mentally. It combats depression, lethargy and illness. It helps to foster an active, positive attitude towards all aspects of life, not only personal health but also relationships, work and so on.

Causes of unfitness

By contrast, most of us do have some idea of what being unfit means. Breathlessness, irritability, minor aches and pains, obesity, recurring illness, insomnia, are just some of the more obvious symptoms. A general feeling of being out of condition might be another. And there are other symptoms too that are far less obvious such as raised blood pressure or hardening of the arteries.

Despite the health and fitness boom of the last few years, large numbers of women in our society are unfit. Inactivity and stress are probably the two chief reasons. Smoking, alcohol, overeating, inadequate diet and general self-neglect are other, often closely linked, reasons.

Lack of exercise is a prime cause of illness. To some extent, it has to do with the society we live in – cars, trains, buses, lifts, labour-saving devices, sedentary occupations all contribute to the fact that most of us get less exercise than we need. It also has to do with the very fact that we are women, and that women, as we explain later on (see page 48), tend to be much less physically active than men, in terms of sport anyway. It's a part of our conditioning; even today really vigorous exercise, the sort that makes you sweat – and that's what running does – is still seen, quite wrongly, as not really suitable for women. Whatever the reason, however, if the body is not used and exercised to its full potential, it will decline. Like any under-used neglected machine, an under-used body ceases to function efficiently, key organs weaken, and it becomes prey to all sorts of dangers. Lack of exercise shortens life.

Stress too is a major cause of unfitness. Effectively, stress is tension. It is a common feature of our society, and to a greater or lesser extent affects all of us whether we know it or not. But before talking about the physical effects of stress, it is important to look at the stresses that women suffer to understand just why so many women feel 'freedom and enjoyment' in running.

Women in our society are under continual stress, much of it caused by society's expectations of what women should be; we rarely get the opportunity to be ourselves; instead we spend most of our lives trying to live up to these expectations. Even today, despite changes, a women's primary role is to be wife and mother. For instance, we are expected to stay at home, to take on everybody else's problems, understand them, but never to have problems of our own. The woman with small children is on the go twenty-four hours a day, meeting continual demands. There are very few local authority nurseries so the responsibilities are hers and she must never complain. For all the rewards, it can be a lonely, frustrating and isolating job, and one that is rarely appreciated. The very titles 'housewife' and 'working mother' indicate just how little home and childcare are recognised as work in their own right. And mothers are so often to blame if anything goes wrong with the children; it is very easy for a woman to feel guilt – after all it is only a perfect mother who can produce perfect children!

There are very few outlets for women with young children. Instead the home, the children's needs, the husband's needs, the endless domestic drudgery are supposed to provide all the fulfilment necessary. To moan is to be a nag, to pursue our own interests is to be regarded, even today, as selfish, or neglectful of our responsibilities. And for the woman who does devote all her energies to the home, stress increases when the children leave. In later age, then, many women find themselves isolated, without friends or outside interests, frequently lacking the necessary confidence to go out and find new outlets and pursuits.

Nora, for instance, found herself isolated and lonely when her husband died. She started jogging on Easter Sunday 1984 at the age of sixty-two. It is best described in her own words:

'I found jogging very easy from the start, but I have been doing aerobics for one and a half years . . . also keep fit class for the last twenty years but that is not strenuous. I started jogging because I had to do something to keep me from the utter loneliness after my husband died . . . it saved me from a lot of misery and depression which I know would have hit me if I had not struck out straight away. I must admit the social side to all this plays a major part not only on the runs but whenever you meet any one of these men and women. The benefits are enormous, feeling good, looking good, trim figure, good appetite, lots more all round confidence and being able to help people in a situation as mine, watching them look and feel better. Everybody supports me in my running and gives me lots of encouragement.

Nora finishes her story by saying 'long may we run!' Nor is life any easier for the woman who rejects or is forced to abandon the stereotype of the happily-married woman at home. Single parents, waged women, lesbians and disabled women, among others, all face special and individual problems. The waged mother, for instance, carries a double burden: responsibility for a waged job and for the demands of a home and family – two full-time jobs rolled into one. The single parent is now recognised as one of the most impoverished members of our society, while the woman who rejects husband and family to achieve complete 'independence' through waged employment is almost inevitably under more stress than most men, merely by virtue of being a woman and constantly having to prove her worth in a 'man's' world: the world of work. Gay women too may face isolation – no matter how many changes have occurred in the last few years, the rejection of stereotyped heterosexuality is not always greeted sympathetically, and loneliness, deception and the fear of rejection can be a real problem for many gay women.

Even health itself may become a pressure on women. The last few years have seen a veritable 'fitness explosion' but for women, advertised fitness tends to come in a leotard-wrapped package that also includes the 'right' sort of body, dress and appearance. The corsetted, restricted ideal of Victorian womanhood may have been left behind, but she has only been replaced by another ultra feminine stereotype, the slim, beautiful and unflappable woman. So that when exercise or a healthy diet are promoted it is too often in the name of beauty rather than fitness, so that exercise itself becomes yet another pressure.

These then are some of the tensions that we suffer, made worse by the fact that as women we rarely have the confidence to challenge or confront what is happening to us. So often we don't even realise that we are in a stressful situation. As women we often internalise stress because we lack the necessary assertion skills to express ourselves, or to make others understand how we feel. And the effects can be devastating. The fact is that stressful situations may be one-offs, or they may be prolonged, but depending on our ability to cope with them, the immediate effects on the body are the same. Faced with a stressful situation, the muscles tense, heart and breathing rates increase, powerful hormones – adrenaline and noradrenalin – are released, the liver excretes sugar and fatty acids, and the entire body prepares itself for emergency action in what is known as the 'fight or flight' syndrome. It is a very primitive defence mechanism but unfortunately, today, physical action is rarely appropriate. We can't fight the situation, nor can we run away. Instead we internalise stress. As women we are not supposed to lose our tempers, act out our aggression, express our true emotions; instead we have to keep them curbed, and the unexpressed emotions lead to, among other things, nervous headaches, nervous indigestion, an inability to relax, perhaps even severe depression, neuroses or drug dependence. At the same time, the fatty acids and sugars released into the bloodstream, if not burned up by exercise, may turn into cholesterol, leading to circulatory disorders such as atherosclerosis and other circulatory disorders. Over prolonged periods of time, then, unresolved stress simply wears the body out.

So – why running?

It's quite simple really, running makes you feel good. It combats stress, provides an outlet for tension, and gives us confidence in ourselves. At a fundamental physical level, running does you good. As we describe later (see page 89) running is an aerobic exercise that improves the overall efficiency of the body, and in particular the heart and lungs, the key elements of fitness. Women runners have also found that among other things running helps them to sleep better, eases migraines, tension headaches and period pains. No wonder then that jogging has a four-star rating from the British Health Education Council.

But, physical fitness apart, running brings confidence to women; the confidence we acquire as we build up our mileage, proving to ourselves just what we are capable of. For a human species that has been told all her life that strenuous activity is unladylike, running provides a massive release and sense of achievement.

And it's cheap – a crucial factor for many women. It doesn't cost very much to run – you don't have to buy a tennis racket, book and pay for a tennis court. The only financial investment you may have to make is the price of a pair of running shoes. And you can run anywhere and at any time you want to. You can run on the streets, around the block, in the park, through fields or woods; whatever your particular environment, you can find somewhere to run.

Running is a social occasion too. You can run on your own, but many women like to run with other women. It gives us a chance to talk and laugh with other women, away from continual demands, stress or loneliness. As Nora found, it can even be a means of meeting new people and of making friends, through running clubs, entering fun runs, or even starting your own running groups.

Age doesn't matter either; women of all ages are running today. Mary was fifty-nine when she started running; Nora was sixty-two. Provided you have some basic fitness, anyone can run. Nor do you need to be 'good'; there is no good and bad running, there's only running.

These are very important advantages for women but there are more: running gives women the benefits and rewards that in our daily life seem so inconceivable and impossible. For me, running has brought together all the ideas of liberation for women in one action, providing a way out of our lack of confidence and assertiveness, our feelings of insecurity and low self-esteem. We as women want to feel strong and in control of our bodies; we want to be able to cope. It's not just in my imagination when I think, and other women say, that running provides 'Fitness in mind and body . . . relaxation of mind, calmness, a reduction in stress, sanity and an emotional high'.

To some people 10 miles or more sounds like purgatory. It did to me at first but now, to me and many other women runners, it's a wonderful feeling of freedom, liberation, nirvana reached through actual bodily movements, moving limbs, legs, arms, and breathing in rhythm, in tune with yourself. Running is the best thing that has happened to me; for me and for other women, running has opened new doors, given us a new understanding of ourselves, euphoria and a peace of mind that most people associate with passive meditation.

It is true that running gives you a happy feeling; it is no wonder that one woman says that for her running is 'a cure for depression, a means of more energy and fun'. Some people have suggested that there may be a chemical basis for the addiction that running brings. This may or may not be so, but there is no doubt that running can become a positive addiction as you get into a rhythm that creates that wonderful effortless feeling of floating, when legs and feet feel way away from the head. It is during these moments of effortless running that any problems that might have bothered you before you went out seem to have dissolved as the sweat trickles down your skin – of course it's not magic and problems are still there but the burden has gone.

3 WOMEN WITH DISABILITIES

I know I'm fit to run this race
Forgive me if I'm blue in face
I'm epileptic as you see
So please don't worry about me
Take me to the race's end
And in an hour or two I'll mend
And then I'll meet my friends all tired
It's sad my brain's wrongly wired

Val was inspired to write this poem when she took part in her first marathon – the London Marathon. She wrote it on the back of the number that was pinned to her front during the race. It is the place where you write any disability you might suffer during the race. Appropriately enough, however, as Val fights against the label of disability, no-one would ever have known: by the time she arrived at the finish, sweat had rubbed the poem off.

Val is thirty-nine years old with two children aged ten and thirteen. She began running after watching her husband compete in the first London Marathon. Although her husband had been running for some time, it never occurred to Val to start, but watching the runners she was inspired:

> 'It was seeing these people run, being at the beginning, the middle, the end, Greenwich, Tower Bridge, to where it finished. And I saw all sorts and all ages . . . and I was most inspired and impressed by them, and very proud of the individual's triumph, in whatever time, in whatever condition. And I started running after that.'

Val's husband had suggested that she take up running because it would be something they could do together. She already played badminton, cycled and swam, but it took her twenty attempts to run three-quarters of a mile without 'wingeing', her chest and limbs hurt so much. She found the entire experience very uncomfortable, and decided not to continue. However, her husband suggested that she invest in a pair of running shoes. These turned out to be '£27-worth of responsibility' on her feet, and she felt she had to try harder. The shoes were comfortable, much better than the old trainers she had worn before. The turning point was when she found another woman friend to run with. As she says:

'For six weeks during June and July and before the summer holidays started, I got up in the morning because she was expecting me at 7 o'clock, and she got up because she was expecting me, and we ran through the woods for about half an hour. I have never regained the joy and freedom of movement, and have never got up at 7 o'clock since. But for six weeks we did, mutually dependent on each other to get up. The woods are at the end of our gardens and it was beautiful.'

For Val this 'broke the back of it', and she moved on to longer distances, running a 5½-mile route round the town. Today, although she runs less regularly, she can run 10 miles in 85 minutes as and when she wants to.

Some months later in the autumn of that same year, and when she had completed her first marathon, Val started a club for runners. Initially it was for women only because, as Val says: 'I know women are so afraid to be seen and so afraid at having to wear shorts and things.' The club, which does not include men, meets three times a week, and attracts runners of quite differing abilities. Club runs vary in distance so that club members can run for as long or as short a distance as they wish. The shortest run is Val's troublesome three-quarter-mile. What Val is most concerned with is 'people not hurting themselves and being put off, and I'm concerned that they don't do too much and are discouraged. So I'm concerned that what they aim for is within their ability, that they have support'. Val recommends that new runners should invest in a good pair of running shoes to avoid injury.

Val knows for her and other women

'the benefits are multi-various. I am fit, I am bouncy, I have more friends, I am part of a club. I run because I can, because I see my friends because lots of us have taken it up since I did, and I am pleased with my increased energy and stamina. I get long days of improved health. I can now run 10 miles, have a shower, have a sandwich and go on and do the next thing with the day. And I think my running, my fitness, my stamina, is a self-sustaining, self-producing form of energy, not a waste of energy.'

This differs from Val's mother's idea of how she should use her energy. 'My mother thinks it is a waste of energy, and that I should be using my energy to clean the oven', but Val knows she's 'not an oven cleaner anyway. . . . I am saying that it is not a waste of energy because my running has produced more energy'. For Val one of the best things is that 'I can put on my training shoes and run anywhere'. Running, she says, has also increased her stamina for other sports: she can now stay on the squash court for one and a half hours.

Val had her first major epileptic fit at the age of twenty-one; since then she has had fifteen more. Val recalls:

'My mother took it very badly when I had this epilepsy, people do suffer more vicariously through their children. . . . I mean laughing it off is quite the wrong thing for my mother. . . . I don't know how it has affected me really, I just know that if anyone says I'm not able because of it, I could give them a big list of things I have achieved over the last eighteen years since I was diagnosed. It's given me this bigger drive to help others, I get satisfaction out of that, but it also proves that my epilepsy is only relative.'

That's why Val wrote the poem on the back of her London Marathon number. She now has warning signs before a fit, can't speak as fast and can't get to the end of sentences.

Val is not as worried about her epilepsy as she is 'at being labelled disabled. . . . I work harder to prove that I'm alright. . . . I work very hard because I am frightened of people's sympathy and probably just as frightened of their admiration'.

Val has done the second, third and fourth London Marathons. She ran the last one for a school in Hertfordshire for epileptic children.

Val not only did the last London Marathon to raise money but also to prove that she was running for herself and not her husband. At the moment Val is going through a traumatic period. Having once achieved a marathon she felt she could 'harness' her body to do anything, and subsequently went deep-sea diving. With her new-found physical ability, she became more assertive and her husband, not liking this new person, took off, leaving her and their daughter. Of this troubled time Val says:

'To be fit is to be confident and to be able to do a marathon during the troubled time which I've had lately has given me confidence. It has given me some pleasure that I could still run a marathon. I was at my heaviest weight, and had done less training, but I managed my best time . . . and I'm pleased to run. . . . I believe if women can conquer this hurdle, we can do anything.'

Val has epilepsy – a disorder of the nervous system, symptoms of which may include convulsions and loss of consciousness, something that alarms others. And yet Val runs. Asthma – a disorder which affects the bronchial tubes – can also produce alarming symptoms. And I know at least two women runners who suffer from asthma, Eileen Buckley and Caroline Rodgers, one of our top runners. Both were recommended by doctors to take up exercise, and both took up running. Eileen began running in her thirties and has felt a lot better since. She feels more relaxed; the cold air affects her but even in cold weather she just carries on running. In fact when I first ran with Eileen, I didn't know she was an asthma sufferer; she did amazingly well and never sounded distressed.

When Caroline was twenty-one she was encouraged by her doctor to take up sport. She was having frequent asthma attacks because she had just moved to London and didn't know anybody. Her doctor thought sport would not only help her asthma, but also would be a way of making new friends. So she joined the Highgate Harriers first as a sprinter and then moved up to longer distances. In 1976 she ran in the first UK women-only marathon held in Feltham, London. All the women achieved remarkable times – the first three women completed the run in under 3 hours. Caroline came third with a time of 2 hours 58 minutes. She found it very hard and vowed never to do another one, but has since succumbed and her personal best (p.b.) now stands at 2 hours 44 minutes 17 seconds. Both Caroline and Eileen find Intal inhailer, used in cases where asthma is related to allergy, the best aid and both take it before running. Caroline did experiment once and tried to run without it, but only got as far as the end of the road and returned very wheezy. On one occasion she forgot to take her Intal and couldn't understand why she felt so wheezy a mile before she reached the track.

I have also run with a woman who suffers with diabetes – a disorder in which the pancreas fails to produce sufficient glucose. I remember the two of us doing a track race together, and just as we were warming up she started chewing a sweet – an unusual thing to do just before a race – and then she told me that she was diabetic. She had also run a marathon, so, as with asthma and epilepsy, it is also possible to run with diabetes, although it is important to get medical advice before starting, and to maintain strict attention to diet.

Sport doesn't come easily

These women are women with disabilities that would probably pass unnoticed by others. By contrast there are many women with more noticeable disabilities such as lack of limb, sight or hearing, or women perhaps confined to wheelchairs. Such women are rarely accepted as 'normal' in their daily life, but being accepted in sports circles is even harder and more of a struggle. There are certainly no role models for such women.

Being a disabled sportswoman is not a glamorous situation; the rewards come entirely from personal achievement and success; there is absolutely no public recognition. The media ignores sportswomen at the best of times but how much coverage did we see of the disabled Olympics (the International Games for the Disabled) held in New York, or of the 1984 Paralympics held in Stoke Mandeville, UK? We had about an hour of New York, (although the Americans showed all the events on cable television), and I must have blinked and missed the Paralympics! (An hour was actually shown on British television.)

Medical classification for athletes with disabilities

Athletes with disabilities are divided into seven categories – paraplegic (or spinal injuries); deaf; visually handicapped; mentally handicapped; cerebral palsy; amputee; and Les Autres (The Others). This last category includes a wide range of disabilities such as multiple sclerosis, muscular dystrophy, thalidomide, spina bifida, arthritis and so on.

Each category in turn has a medical classification for different events, according to the degree of disability. For example, an ambulant person (someone who can move around on one or two legs) would be in a different classification from a person in a wheelchair.

Wheelchair runners usually start 5 minutes before able-bodied runners in any road race that they are 'allowed' to compete in. This is mainly for safety. The wheelchairs used have large wheels, small handrims, and low-slung seats, and there are various types of chairs depending on the disability. These chairs weigh about 17lbs compared with an ordinary wheelchair which is about 40lbs.

An athlete in her own right

Kim White is confined to a wheelchair but is a world-class athlete – she competed in the 1984 International Games for the Disabled in New York. She is a thrower rather than a runner, but will be taking up running because she intends to take part in the pentathlon which will be introduced in the next disabled Olympics due to be held in 1988 at Seoul, South Korea, one month before the able-bodied Olympics.

In 1979 Kim had an operation on her knee – she went into hospital with a walking stick and came out with crutches and a wheelchair. She was depressed and went to stay with her sister, and it was while she was there, watching a disabled sportsman at a local event, that she became interested and decided to take up sport. She tried out various events and was successful but it was two years before anyone would accept her. There is a lot of discrimination in sports clubs. As Kim says of that two-year fight for acceptance: 'There are two battles – we're fighting the fact that we're women in sport, and the fact that we're disabled and have got wheelchairs . . . .' Finally, however, she was successful and in 1984 went to the New York Games.

As Kim points out, at present the title 'Olympics' applies only to the able-bodied games, although President Reagan apparently told the disabled athletes that they had been accepted by the Olympic governing body, and at New York their games were officially opened with the Olympic flag and torch. This ceremony is very important to disabled athletes. As Kim describes: 'We're athletes in our own right which is what we have been fighting for. . . . I don't see why the Olympics should be just for the able-bodied. If you're the world's best in your class, why shouldn't you have recognition the same as anybody else?'

The good thing is that in 1988 the disabled will be using the same track and facilities as the able-bodied, and the games for disabled athletes will be held a month earlier. The Olympics for the disabled takes time. Wheelchair discus throwers, for instance, have to be strapped in each time they throw; blind runners run individually (with a partner), while ambulant runners take longer than their able-bodied counterparts.

Money is one of the biggest problems, especially for wheelchair athletes. As Kim says: 'The majority of us that went to America have overdrafts on our overdrafts. You need twelve months to clear expenses, and you still have to think of the next year's expenses.' Kim and her husband, John, worked out their expenses for next year: training, training weekends, plus a couple of competitions, will cost £800 or more, and that is without equipment and the wear and tear on their car. Her husband also has to take time off work, give up his overtime, and move his shift around.

The British Sports Association for the Disabled (BSAD) approached the British Sports Aid Foundation for financial support for Kim, but their request was turned down. In all the Foundation was approached three times, and each time turned down the request on the grounds that Kim was too old (she is forty-six). Of this Kim says: 'They need educating; disabled athletes go on competing until they are a lot older. Even though I have been to America and brought back medals, they still think I am too old . . .' In the end Kim's local newspaper set up a fund for her to go.

For Kim and so many other disabled athletes, sport relieves the frustration and tensions of being in a wheelchair. The enjoyments are the various personal achievements, meeting other people and exchanging views. As well there is the sensation of being at the peak of physical performance and, of course, the knowledge that 'you can actually do it'. Set against these, however, are massive problems of prejudice and discrimination.

It's not all downhill

Denise and Karen are wheelchair runners with personal bests for the marathon of 3 hours 35 minutes 30 seconds and 3 hours 58 minutes 37 seconds respectively. Denise came in second woman and eighth overall in the 1984 National Wheelchair Marathon championships, held in conjunction with the Gloucester Marathon, and Karen came in third woman and eleventh overall.

Denise was a swimmer before taking up wheelchair running four years ago. She saw an advertisement for anyone interested in running, and asked whether wheelchairs were allowed. They were. The following year she invited another wheelchair user along, and in 1984, with other wheelchair runners, instigated the first National Wheelchair Marathon.

Denise had polio as a child but her predicament was made even worse by a car accident five years ago which left her without the use of her lower limbs. As a result she is completely chairbound. Denise lives on her own, and has a full-time job which she feels she has to be very good at because disabled people are discriminated against, and Denise feels she must prove she can cope as well as an able-bodied person. (Personally I think she copes better than many able-bodies.)

Keeping fit is important to Denise, it helps her to cope with work; at the same time she has to go to work to keep fit, after all, money is important. Wheelchairs are expensive – the most expensive British wheelchair costs about £900 compared with the price of a good pair of running shoes! Even before she saw the running advertisement, she had done some wheelchair running to supplement her swimming. She says that wheelchair running uses the cardio-vascular system in the same way as able-bodied running. 'I train between 30 to 50 miles a week, depending on the weather, and I also do flexibility work. I occasionally do weights to balance the other muscles but I find that I do enough weight training lifting my own body weight around.' Initially Denise wanted to train with an athletic club so got in touch with the Aldershot, Farnham and District. However, they said they only had limited track facilities so she now trains with Reading Athletic Club and joins them on their training nights.

Karen too was a swimmer, a competitive swimmer, before she started running but has now given it up in favour of running. She was initially influenced into sport by watching a half-hour programme on the International Games for the Disabled about four years ago. She decided to attempt a marathon because, she says, 'I wanted to show other people what I can do'. But she had to get a special racing chair which arrived only five days before the event, namely the National Wheelchair Championship, so that was all the time she had for training. Karen only managed 15 miles of training before the marathon. On the day itself she says, 'I was tired after the first five miles, and exhausted after 16, but I carried on to the finish'. In the event she achieved the remarkable time of 3 hours 58 minutes 37 seconds for her first-ever marathon, and after only 15 miles of training (not to be recommended for everyone).

Both Karen and Denise wish that wheelchair athletes were treated as equals with able-bodied athletes. After all, Denise says, 'Training is hard; it's not all downhill. We have the same ability to train and run'. And she hopes that they will be welcomed to races in the future as their campaign grows. She commented: 'The first London Marathon was very unfriendly, very different from the Great North Run where there are no problems. Now, however, the London does welcome wheelchair athletes.'

Denis buys *Running*, a British magazine for the able-bodied, so that she knows what is going on, but unless disabled runners produce their own articles, no reference is made to wheelchair runners. By contrast, there is a magazine in the United States called *Sports and Spokes*. Also, about the United States, Denise says, 'There . . . we are taken seriously and are sponsored which doesn't happen here'. However, a British National Wheelchair Road Running Committe has now been formed which is part of the BSAD so Denise hopes that 'people will finally sit up and take notice'.

Problems

From the previous stories it is obvious that disabled women athletes face many problems. Prejudice is the greatest – sport for the disabled is a neglected area, and disabled sportswomen are ignored or excluded from events and facilities even more than able-bodied sportswomen. Able-bodied athletes can do a great deal to help in understanding the needs and problems of disabled athletes and by offering encouragement and giving recognition, to add their efforts to push for change.

Running and other clubs must recognise, welcome and encourage women with disabilities. Facilities and training sessions must be extended to athletes with disabilities. Each disability has its own practical problems, and these must be catered for. A wheelchair runner, for instance, needs more space on a track than an able-bodied runner and this must be taken into account; synthetic rather than cinder tracks too should be available as should any other specialist equipment required. Blind runners, as another example, need a sighted athlete to run and train with. Deaf runners cannot hear a starting gun, nor can they socialise easily with other, hearing athletes. Yet, how many able-bodied athletes are either present or take the trouble to communicate with deaf athletes before or after a race? Very few able-bodied athletes understand these problems and it is crucial that they do – all women athletes whether disabled or able-bodied have the right to train and participate in sport. Together we must demand this right.

While particular events and equipment must be tailored to suit the needs of disabled women athletes, there should be much more communication between the disabled and able-bodied so that all of us can share our successes and problems. *Running* and other sports magazines should have sections devoted to the athlete or runner with disabilities. While disabled women have their own specific problems, they also share the same general problems with able-bodied women: lack of money and time, difficulties of childcare, periods, sex discrimination, training difficulties and so on. All of us equally as women need the same opportunity to air and share our views, ideas and needs.

Lack of money is a major hurdle. In the United States athletes with disabilities are sponsored. In Britain they are not. The BSAD *needs* more money. Making financial ends meet is a problem for most of us, but disabled women runners have extra expenses, among them racing wheelchairs, the cost of training weekends and getting to races. Sponsorship to cover these needs is essential.

Prejudice, discrimination and lack of money are probably the chief problems facing disabled sportswomen, certainly they were most frequently mentioned by the women we spoke to. Others, such as the difficulties of actually getting to events and bad weather conditions, were also mentioned. There are probably many more and these must be made obvious. The difficulty has been that women with disabilities, like all other women, have been invisible for too long, discriminated against on grounds of sex and disability. We need to force change. Hopefully this section has made a few more people aware of the problems that sportswomen with disabilities have to overcome. There are signs that change is beginning – the British Women's Sports Federation, for instance, clearly recognises the barriers in front of disabled sportswomen and women like Kim, Denise and Karen, by participating, are themselves forcing change. But we need to push for more, and above all for recognition. Running is a means for all women – disabled and able-bodied to get together and make changes. It may or may not be a question of integration, opinions differ, what is important is to remember, as Kim says, that 'we are all athletes in our own right'. Disabled sportswomen don't want sympathy – just recognition.

4 *RUNNING THROUGH TIME*

When we were researching this section at the Sports Council in London, we came across a book by Robert Quercitani calling itself *A World History of Track and Field Athletics 1864-1964*. Published in Britain in 1964, it claimed to be a 'comprehensive' history of the subject and yet in all its 370 pages we found not one single reference to a woman athlete. Some comprehensive history! But in many ways we weren't really surprised; the absence of women in that book just mirrors the way in which, for centuries, women's involvement and achievements in sport have been either ignored or completely trivialised. As far as we can discover, sport, because of its traditional association with the so-called male qualities of virility, competitiveness and aggression, has always been regarded as a masculine activity, not really suitable for women. Historically the sporting world has been predominantly a man's world so that, for thousands of years, sportswomen have been ridiculed, discouraged, ignored or even deliberately excluded from participating. In fact, given all the various obstacles, myths, misconceptions and anti-women prejudices that have abounded in sport, what becomes much more surprising is that any women have participated at all. But, despite their obscurity, women have always taken part in sport, although to do so they have had, more often than not, to risk censure and to rebel against all existing conventions.

Men only

There's nothing new about running – people have always run for one reason or another. But throughout Western history, competitive running events have almost invariably been designed for and dominated by men; women's involvement has depended entirely on the prevailing – and usually sexist – attitudes of the time. For the ancient Greeks physical prowess and masculinity were synonymous; sports were an expression and celebration of male virility and sexuality so that, by definition, athleticism was associated with masculinity. Hardly surprisingly, then, women were excluded from the original Olympic Games; they were not allowed to take part nor were they allowed to watch, death being the penalty for so doing. Then, as now, some women rebelled. In 404BC uproar was caused when it was discovered that Pherenice, widowed mother and trainer of Peisirodus, a young male boxer, was actually in the Olympic stadium disguised as a man to watch her son. Although Pherenice was discovered she fortunately escaped death but only because her father, brothers and son were all Olympic victors.

What is less known, however, is that some Greek women, excluded from the men's Games, held their own athletic events. One festival in particular – the Heraea – was actually held at Olympia. Organisers and participants were women and the festivals, held once every four years, included a 160m sprint for girls as well as other running events. Unfortunately, and unlike the all-male Olympics, we know very little about the Heraea or any other of the women's athletic events apparently held at the time, although it would seem as if a women's reputation suffered as a result of participating – hardly surprising in a patriarchal society where a woman's place was in the home.

Only in one instance were women actively encouraged to take part in sport. Spartan women were trained from girlhood in running and various other sporting activities. Their training, however, was not for their own sakes but was designed to develop their health and stamina in order that they should produce fine sons to become great Spartan warriors. Significantly, while the male winners of the Olympic Games became political and religious heroes, honoured for life, often supported from public funds and even, on occasion, promised 'a beautiful and good woman' as a reward, the female Spartan athlete was regarded purely as a more efficient breeding machine.

Government warning: sport can damage your health

Just as sport has traditionally been a male domain, so too, and throughout history, women have been regarded as too passive or delicate to participate. Although, finally, Roman women were admitted to the ancient Olympics, needless to say their function was to watch and cheer the male athletes, a remarkably familiar role to any women who have stood in the cold watching lovers, brothers, sons or husbands running around a football pitch.

This same pattern of active male/passive female has been repeated time and time again, influencing women's involvement in sport, and reaching its height perhaps during the Victorian era when the cult of femininity attained what seems to us now ludicrous proportions. For the Victorians the ideal, 'feminine' woman was not only subordinate but also far too frail to be anything but a good wife and mother. Physical exertion for such fragile beings was not only socially unthinkable, it was also considered to be seriously damaging to a woman's health. In the mid-nineteenth century, a British government report specifically stated that 'games' for girls would lead to flat-chestedness and impaired reproductive abilities while at the same time the male-dominated medical profession on both sides of the Atlantic preached the dangers for women of any strenuous activity whether physical or mental. The argument put forward was that the human body had only limited reserves of energy. Women, it was argued, needed to conserve all their energy to meet the physical demands of their bodies, namely menstruation and reproduction. To do otherwise, to 'waste' energy on sport, or even education, was to risk damage to the ovaries, the uterus, and even to the unborn child. As a result, therefore, women were exhorted to conserve their energies, particularly at puberty and during and after pregnancy.

For women and young girls then inactivity and ill-health were the order of the day. While boys were encouraged to run, to play ball, and to develop speed, stamina and agility, girls were expected to be 'ladylike' and passive, restricted to such gentle pastimes as hoop-rolling, occasional 'bathing', croquet and ice skating, although even here female skaters were urged to hang onto their male partners' coat tails so that they could be pulled around without too much effort. And what social attitudes began, clothing and fashion continued, women's physical lives being further restricted by the corsets, tight lacing, stays and cumbersome clothing of the period.

The net result of all this was to create a society in which delicacy and inactivity were the norm for most women. To be 'feminine' was to be frail, to be passive was 'ladylike'. But it was an image imposed primarily on middle-class women who above all were expected to be showcases for their husband's newly-acquired wealth. Women of the upper classes were less bound by such genteel restrictions and had always enjoyed comparatively more freedom to follow such traditional pursuits as fox hunting and other field sports. Nor was it an ideal appropriate to working and labouring women, such as those employed in the mines or the mills, whose lives of physical drudgery meant that they were regarded as 'unfeminine' anyway, and who had little if any time for recreation, a pattern just as common today.

Bicycles and bloomers

Fortunately women can't be kept down for ever and from the late nineteenth century, increasing numbers began to throw off the twin shackles of corsets and frailty in order to take up sports. In part this was due to the effects of industrialism which placed an increasing emphasis on sport as a means of recreation so that women of the leisured middle class began to join their upper-class sisters in newly-acceptable pursuits such as lawn tennis and golf. The advent of higher education for women also had an effect. Both in the United States and Britain, leading advocates of education for women such as Miss Frances Buss and Miss Dorothea Beale countered the old arguments that academic work was damaging to a woman's health by urging the adoption of gentle physical exercise for health and fitness. As a result, from the 1850s, callisthenics (exercises for grace and strength) and Swedish-style gymnastics, both of which were considered suitably 'ladylike', were introduced into the curriculum of new girls' schools such as North London Collegiate, Cheltenham and Roedean. By the turn of the century they were well established, and their therapeutic qualities widely recognised.

In the United States the all-women colleges Vassar and Wellesley adopted a full programme of sports and exercises when they were founded in 1865 and 1876 respectively in an attempt to disprove myths of women's frailty, while from the 1890s basketball too was being played enthusiastically by American college women. In Britain, however, organised outdoor games as played in the boys' public schools were still considered unsuitable for women, but from the 1890s some new 'non-masculine' sports were introduced: hockey, lacrosse, rounders and netball. Track athletics, rowing and swimming were also adopted.

Clothing remained a major obstacle for any woman wishing to participate in sport as, despite the introduction of the gym-slip in 1893, long skirts, stays and stiff buckram still remained the conventional outdoor sporting dress. Feminists and physicians alike blamed corsets and tight lacing for much of the ill-health of Victorian women, naming them as the cause of various disorders ranging from overlapping and fractured ribs to damaged reproductive organs. But despite their warnings, and the arguments of the Rational Dress Society, change was slow until the advent of the bicycle. Invented in the 1870s, the popularity of the bicycle soared between 1890 and 1914 both in the United States and Britain. In 1895, the American feminist, Elizabeth Cady Stanton declared that 'Many a woman is riding to the suffrage on a bicycle' and indeed probably no other machine did more to liberate women before World War I. Organisations like the Boston Women's League, and magazines such as *Punch* warned that cycling would lead women into evil ways. Despite their dire messages, women seized on the bicycle as a means of mobility and independence, finally jettisoning their tight lacing, corsets and petticoats in favour of bloomers and divided skirts – on the move at last.

You can't be an athlete and a woman too

By 1914 then women were entering a wide range of sports and other pursuits from cycling to hockey and swimming. World War I removed further restrictions and the post-war years saw the emergence of an increasing number of sportswomen among them Helen Willis, top female US tennis player between 1923 and 1925, Annette Kellerman, the Australian swimmer, and Gertrude Ederle, cross-Channel swimmer who, in 1926, beat the men's record by two hours. But, and for women there always is a but, change was to a great extent skin-deep, and organised, competitive sport remained a man's world, reinforced by the fact that the institutions and practice of sport were all male-dominated and male-defined. During the nineteenth century there was a fanatical emphasis on games, but the emphasis was still on sport as a manly pastime – the Chariots of Fire syndrome. The games field with its emphasis on discipline, team effort and physical striving was the perfect breeding ground for the perfect, upper-class male, while at the same time the working man was being encouraged to take up organised sport as character forming and a means of manly expression. Either way there was no room for women whether on the playing fields of Eton or in the working men's soccer clubs. Little wonder then that women were encouraged to take up sports that enhanced their femininity, activities such as tennis, swimming or gymnastics that required the so-called feminine qualities of skill, grace and physical co-ordination. Competitiveness, exertion, aggression and physical prowess were still synonymous with masculinity; it was not thought appropriate for women to display them. And any woman who did so ran the risk, then as now, of being considered quasi-masculine or unfeminine.

As a result certain sports were 'feminised' – special basketball rules were introduced, for instance, to minimise roughness, while lawn tennis tournaments were reduced from five to three or even two sets especially for women. Many so-called male sports, however, were considered impossible to modify, among them track and field athletics, including running. Although the earliest attested woman's athletic performance in Europe – a 100-yard race won by Miss Eva Francisco in 13 seconds – had been held in Dublin as early as 1891, athletics for women was still regarded with horror by most people. By definition running is competitive, it also requires stamina, endurance, strength and possibly even pain, all of them considered appropriate to the male but not to the female of the species. The aspiring female athlete found herself in a double-bind; to be a serious competitive athlete meant that she could not be a 'feminine' woman, an attitude still only too common today.

You can play but you can't compete

At the same time the world of competitive sport, then as now, was controlled by men, a situation which has restricted women's athletics to the present day. Despite the formation of the British Women's Amateur Athletic Association in 1927, male-dominated institutions such as the International Amateur Athletic Federation (IAAF), which has controlled women's international athletics since 1936, and the International Olympic Committee (IOC) fiercely opposed female involvement in competitive sport. The arguments were, and always have been, the same. Women who made a serious commitment to competitive sport, it was argued, risked among other things, nervous instability, impaired reproductive organs, immature vaginas, and even spinsterhood! The list was almost endless. As a result, when the Olympic Games were revived in 1896, once again they were for men only; while women's swimming and gymnastics appeared on the programme in 1912, women's track and field events were excluded until 1928. Repeated applications by women were met by outraged male disapproval; Baron de Coubertin, the modern Olympic founder, argued that women's track and field events were not only 'against the laws of nature' but also the 'most unaesthetic sight human eyes could contemplate'. Even as late as 1935 he was saying that 'women have but one task, that of crowning the winner with garlands'. Interestingly, however, a woman had run in the 1896 Olympics. Probably the first-ever woman to finish a marathon, she was a Greek runner called Melopene, and she ran quite unofficially, finishing in about 4½ hours.

...crowning the winner with garlands....

Excluded from the Olympics, then, women athletes held their own international competitions. The first-ever women's international track and field events were held in Monte Carlo in 1921. More than 100 women from five nations took part. The following year 300 women competed from seven countries, and it was decided to set up what were initially known as the Women's World Olympics but subsequently, as a result of male pressure, renamed the Women's World Games. Held every four years until 1934, the number of participating nations eventually reached ten or more, and there were thirteen track events although conventional events such as the 400m and 1500m were shortened to 300m and 1,000m respectively.

In 1928, after years of agitation, women athletes were finally, although grudgingly, admitted to the Olympic Games. In contrast to their own Games, however, the Olympic programme included only five track and field events for women, the longest of which was the 800m and what the male administrators gave with one hand, they took away with the other. The sight of West German Lina Radke collapsing on the track after beating the woman's world record for the 800m – just as so many male athletes have collapsed – so outraged the all-male IOC officials that the race was withdrawn that very same year. Nor was it included again until 1960 which left the 100m as the only women's event until the inclusion of the 200m in 1948.

This setback, plus the ending of the Women's World Games in 1934, pushed women's competitive athletics back into obscurity for some years. Despite the growing emancipation of women socially, politically and economically, between the 1940s and 1960s there were few official outlets for the serious female athlete. While swimming, with the addition of synchronised swimming, riding, ski-ing and tennis became increasingly popular 'acceptable' sports for women, track and field athletics plus team and contact sports were generally regarded as unsuitable. And despite the outstanding performances of various woman athletes, the question of serious competition for women remained highly controversial.

Nevertheless, while the all-male ruling bodies continued to drag their feet, women themselves refused to accept myths of biological inferiority (see page 55), and continued to run whether officially or unofficially. One such woman was the outstanding Dutch athlete, Fanny Blankers-Koehn, who at one time held twelve track and field world records. As a mother of two children she exploded biological myths when she broke world records for the 100m, 220 yards, 800m hurdles and pentathlon, and in 1948, while pregnant, won four Olympic medals. Her achievements as an athlete were remarkable but nevertheless were trivialised by the world's press who, in patronising fashion dubbed her 'The Flying Dutch Housewife'.

From the 1960s, however, things began to change. The emergence of the modern feminist movement, the development of contraception, particularly the pill, and the increasing awareness that vigorous activity, far from being harmful, was actually beneficial, gave women the strength and tools to stand up finally and demand their rights in running as in all other areas. The male administrators of sport, of course, dragged their feet and change was slow. Every track and field event had to be fought for. In 1960 the 800m was finally readmitted to the Olympics. In 1964 the women's 400m was added. But it was in 1967 that the issue of women's long-distance running really hit the headlines when the American Katherine

Switzer ran in the famous, and then all-male, Boston Marathon. She was not the first woman to run it. In 1966 Roberta Gibb Bingay had run, but un-officially because her entry form had been refused. Then, in 1967 Katherine Switzer sent in her application as student K. Switzer. She received her official entry number, and it was not until she had run some distance that the organisers realised she was a woman. Outraged officials attempted to drag her away arguing that it was not only illegal for her to run, but also that it was foolish of her to even think she could complete a marathon. A friend intervened, however, with a hefty body charge and Katherine Switzer successfully completed the course – a major and highly publicised triumph for aspiring women runners. Hardly surprisingly, women were then banned from all US marathons, a ban that was not lifted until 1972. Katherine Switzer herself was promptly thrown out of the Amateur Athletics Union (AAU) on the somewhat petulant grounds that: she had fraudulently entered the race; had run longer than the allowed distance; had run with men; and had run without a chaperone!

Into the eighties

Since the 1970s women have continued to reject anti-women prejudices in order to get fitter, and to participate in sports of all kinds. Despite all obstacles, women's involvement in sport has increased dramatically. Throughout the 1970s new events were continually being added to the programme of international sporting competitions. At the same time, an increasing number of individual and highly popular women stars continue to emerge, among them the javelin throwers Tessa Sanderson and Fatima Whitbread, and the American marathon runner Mikki Gorman who won the woman's section of the Boston Marathon in 1974 and 1977. In 1975 she proved yet again what a nonsense male-generated biological arguments have been by coming second in the New York City Marathon at the age of forty, eight months after producing her first child.

In no other area of sport and fitness have women made greater advances than in running. Over the last few years there has been a virtual 'running revolution' as thousands of women of all ages have taken up this sport for fun, health, relaxation and competition, running through streets, parks and on tracks, gaining strength and fitness through running. While in 1978 only forty-eight women completed a British marathon out of a total of 1,789, by 1983 more than 1,500 or 8 per cent of entrants for the London Marathon were women. In 1972 only seventy-two women turned up to run the New York Mini-Marathon – the first race in the world for women only. In 1977 numbers had swelled to more than 2,000 women, their ages ranging from five to sixty-eight, entrants including several pregnant women and thirty-six mother-daughter teams. And in 1984 the Dublin 10km race had the record entry of 9,500 women, an increase of 1,500 women from the previous year, including not only top women athletes but also fun runners and disabled women.

Since the 1960s women have been running regularly in competition over the mile, 1500m and 3,000m as well as the longer track and road-running events – the 5,000m, the 10,000m and the marathon. Even though the actual ratio of women's participation is far lower than men, more women are running today than ever before whether as fun runners or competitive runners. And what is more, they are improving faster than men. Recent research (see page 62) shows that women are literally catching up men. Already some women have run faster than some men over very long distances such as 50 and 100 miles, and over shorter distances their performances are now only 10-15 per cent behind.

Facts such as these show that women want to run and they want to be taken seriously. But male prejudice runs very deep. One of the greatest struggles for women has been to gain acceptance for long-distance running events; ironically the very events for which women seem to be not only best suited but also far more efficient than men in terms of endurance and flexibility (see page 61). It was only in 1972 that the IAAF finally sanctioned women's marathon running. Yet that very same year, before the 1972 New York City Marathon, the AAU suddenly decided that women would not be allowed to run with men. Instead they were to run separately, beginning their race 10 minutes before the men. The women themselves rejected such blatant discrimination. When the starting gun fired, the women, in protest, sat down behind the starting line, waited for the men's race to begin and then, when the men started, the women ran too. A lawsuit followed against the AAU who finally conceded that women and men might start from a common line at a common gunshot.

The arguments go on. Even as late as 1978 the IOC – all male until 1980 – rejected a proposal to include a 3,000m for women in the Moscow Olympic Games on the grounds that it was 'a little too strenuous for women'. But by the 1980s it was impossible for the entrenched officials to ignore the sheer numbers of women runners, and the remarkable achievements of such women as Norwegian Grete Waitz who equalled the world record in the 1983 London Marathon, and American Joan Benoit who established the new world record of 2 hours 22 minutes 43 seconds in the Boston Marathon. Women had proved their point, and in 1984 both the marathon and the 3,000m were admitted for the first time into the Olympic programme, Joan Benoit becoming the first-ever woman Olympic marathon champion.

Women have run a long way from ancient Greece, and attitudes are changing. As the Swiss runner Gabriela Andersen-Schliess staggered over the finishing line of the 1984 women's Olympic Marathon in Los Angeles, she displayed all the classic and harrowing signs of heat prostration. But she was allowed her right to finish. And, in contrast to 1928 when parsimonious male officials banned the women's 800m, it is unlikely that the women's Olympic Marathon will be banned. Instead it looks as if, finally, women's marathon running is here to stay.

So what of the future? Arguments over women's suitability for the 5,000m and 10,000m continue and they are still not included in the Olympic programme. Women athletes are still trivialised in the media, and still face subtle and not so subtle forms of discrimination. But women athletes have discovered their strength and confidence and women runners are not going to give up what they have fought so hard for. Even so, to quote the American magazine *Runner's World*, 'no matter how well a woman runs she will never get the attention she deserves if she's back in a pack of men'. This is especially true of competitive running events where women's achievements are still frequently unrecognised and often overshadowed by the achievements of men. The question should be asked now whether there should be separate women's championships so that women can be recognised on their own terms and not be judged by, and compared with, men.

5 RUNNING ON THE SPOT: HOW IT IS TODAY

Sportswomen face continual discrimination. Basically, sport is a male sphere – through governing bodies, agencies, sports promoters, the media and even in sports magazines themselves, sportswomen are trivialised and patronised.

Doing research for this book we constantly found statements such as women 'were not allowed' to compete in such and such an event, or women 'were allowed' on a given date to compete in a given event. Who says so? In the 1984 Olympics women were 'allowed' to run the marathon for the first time, but weren't 'allowed' to run the 5,000m or the 10,000m or to do the steeplechase. At the Olympics, there are 168 all-male events, and only seventy-three all-women events. In both summer and winter Olympics women only make up 20 per cent of all competitors.

This imbalance is not surprising. The founder of the modern Olympics and the then President of the International Olympic Committee (IOC) was Pierre de Coubertin who was renowned for his opposition to women in sport. Although he resigned in 1928, the IOC is still male-dominated: it is made up of eighty-six men to only three women, and, to a great extent, it still carries on Coubertin's ideals. The National Olympic Committee too and the Federation of Sport (which propose new Olympic events) are also male-dominated; their roots lie in the British public schools, and this aristocratic male tradition still permeates such committees. There have been a few sympathetic men, notably the former IOC President, Lord Killanin who, in 1972, campaigned vigorously and against fierce opposition to get a woman elected to the IOC. Needless to say, it took nine years for the first woman to be elected!

To compete in the Olympics is the ultimate dream for most athletes, but for sportswomen this means that we have had to wait around, or in many cases are still waiting around, for some 'benevolent, liberal-minded men' (to quote Jennifer Hargreaves) to 'allow' us to compete in events for which we are very well suited. This has in fact happened recently during the American Olympic trials and was reported in the September 1984 issue of the American magazine *Runner's World*. Primo Nebiolo of Italy, head of the International Amateur Athletic Federation (IAAF), was watching the trials and was asked by a reporter whether a 5,000m and 10,000m would be included for women in the Olympics, as there were exhibition races put on for the trials. Nebiolo's assistant, Lucian Barro answered and what he ultimately said was no. Yes, 'the IAAF will recommend and the IOC will grant a woman's 10,000m for 1988' but there will not be a 5,000m as 'there just isn't enough talent to justify it'.

More to the point it seems that these benevolent men have already granted women the 3,000m and the marathon – so what else do we want? In the same issue of *Runner's World* journalist Dan Ferrara explains that a law suit was taken out against the IAAF 'on behalf of eighty-two women, no longer asking for but now demanding equal opportunity in the Games'. Lucky IAAF. A Los Angeles court dismissed the final appeal, and the issue died in the middle of the trials. The women's world record for the 5,000m held by Ingrid Kristiansen of Norway now stands at 14 minutes 58 seconds. The talent is obviously there. So why the objections? Male pride? Dan Ferrara goes on to quote ex-marathon runner Jacqueline Hansen who brought the lawsuit. She comments '. . . They kept expecting us to be grateful for the 3,000m and the marathon . . . their attitude about the suit is that we're biting the hand that fed us . . .'.

At this level of competitive athletics, too, not only are women in general discriminated against but also on a global scale women are grossly unrepresented or under-represented at the Olympics. Asian women and women from Islamic countries are almost entirely unknown. Not only is the IOC male-dominated but also the African, Latin American, Asian and Arab nations, where women are bound by profound cultural and religious restrictions, hold a considerable chunk of the voting power. As a result they have so far managed to prevent almost completely the participation of women athletes from these countries.

In 1972 the United States Congress enacted an Education Amendment Act. Within it the so-called Title IX stated that: 'No person in the United States shall, on the basis of sex, be excluded from participation, be denied the benefits of, or be subjected to, any discrimination under an educational program or activity receiving federal financial assistance', a statement of equality reinforced in 1975 by the Department of Health, Education and Welfare's call for 'equal athletic opportunities for both sexes'. Since then, although there have been hiccups, sports programmes sponsored by organisations receiving federal funds have had to show proof of equal opportunities for women and men. And within American schools, anyway, young women are receiving sporting opportunities previously unknown.

In Britain, however, the 1975 Sex Discrimination Act, although it has done sterling work in other areas, does much less to promote equality in competitive sport. Section 44 of the Act states quite explicitly that it is still legal to exclude women from '. . . any sport, game or other activity of a competitive nature where the physical strength, stamina or physique of the average woman puts her at a disadvantage to the average man . . .'. The onus of proof rests on the woman, and the Act makes no attempt to define what is meant by 'average woman' or 'disadvantage'. Even so it doesn't take much imagination to work it out. The Act has been tested on a number of occasions, most notably in the case of Theresa Bennett, a then eleven year old girl and talented footballer who in 1978 went to court because the Football Association had refused her permission to play in one of their teams. The Court upheld the FA's decision on the grounds, among others, that the law would be '. . . exposing itself to absurdity . . . if it tried to make girls into boys so that they could play in a football league . . .' (Lord Denning). Perhaps it is worth remembering that Oscar Wilde once said 'Football is all very well as a game for rough girls but it is hardly suitable for delicate boys'. What more needs to be said?

The attitudes continue; women apparently pose a threat and are even treated with contempt if found competing successfully in this supposed male preserve. Sportswomen are the prey of the media men, and are judged by their image rather than their ability. Women are running today, top women are breaking world records, yet the media continues to trivialise and patronise.

The 1984 Los Angeles Games saw the first-ever women's Olympic Marathon, and yet the only preview information given in that week's British *Radio Times* was one small paragraph:

> Nothing would please the family more were either Grete Waitz or Ingrid Kristiansen to become the first Olympic marathon champion of their sex. The outcome of this contest between the pride of Norway's mothers will take about two and a half hours to deliver.

Can you recognise two serious women athletes in this mish-mash of maternity metaphors?

As it happens, that issue of the *Radio Times* did dedicate some space to women's sports – a descriptive feature on synchronised swimming coyly entitled 'Synch and Swim' in which it was said that appearance counts for a lot in a sport that is largely about grace and beauty of movement, which could be a reason that it hasn't caught on with men ... Carolyn and Caroline will be retiring afterwards so that they can enjoy a normal existence after dedicating themselves to their sport for the last twelve years.

Obviously the BBC considers firstly that synchronised swimming is more appropriate for women than running and, secondly, that a woman's 'normal' existence should be outside sport altogether!

By contrast the next week's *Radio Times* (12 August 1984) devoted an entire page to the men's Olympic marathon, using terms such as 'stoic', 'drama', 'challenge' and providing a much more detailed account of distances, competitors, and even a description of the best way to run a marathon by marathon runner Charlie Spedding. Ironically this same issue finally made reference to the fact that the marathon was a first for women, and listed various competitors. Very good. However, by this time the women's marathon had already taken place and we knew the results!

The television coverage and commentary were little better. British coverage of the women's marathon was continually interrupted by footage of male sport, notably motorcycle racing. There were continual references to 'girls' rather than 'women' or just plain 'athletes/runners', and some of British TV commentator Ron Pickering's comments were belittling to say the least. Describing Joan Benoit, the ultimate winner who was wearing a peaked cap against the sun, he said 'Push that cap sideways, stick a pipe in her mouth, she'd look more like Popeye'. It's unlikely that Ron Pickering could run a marathon with the same ease that Joan Benoit did.

Nice legs, shame about the face

Newspapers and magazines are just as guilty. A particularly nasty slur appeared in the British *News of the World* (22 and 29 July 1984) under the heading 'Marea Hartman Tells All'. Marea Hartman is the Honorary Secretary of the Women's Amateur Athletic Association (WAAA) and Olympic women's team manager. The article consisted of stories and gossip about British top women athletes, who were variously described as being 'deceptively big around the bum', or having 'no bosoms to speak of'. Referring to 'my girls', Marea Hartman said they 'might look masculine on the track – but don't be fooled. Once they've washed their hair and put on their make-up they're a superb lot'. She also refers to the 'coloured girls in our team'. Which colour one wonders? Discussing a particular athlete, she describes how she 'wanders nude wherever we go'. The article goes on, 'most of our girls are a sexy lot. . . . People may hate my guts – but there's no way I'll ever lower my standards . . .'. One of the athletes referred to was in turn interviewed in the British newspaper, The *Guardian* (8 August 1984), and refuted the feature saying: 'It was all disgusting stuff, and all untrue.' The magazine *Athletics Weekly* asked for a public explanation but as yet none has been given.

There is no excuse for this type of article, but unfortunately articles written by sports reporters themselves lead the way to such rubbish. For instance, an article which appeared in *Athlete's World* (January 1983) stated that 'athletes in Britain are quite capable of racing at the highest levels while still retaining their femininity'. Describing the British 800m runner Lorraine Baker, the article went on to say that she combines her running 'with quite startling beauty which would belie her sporting prowess . . .'. Such articles turn a track or road race into nothing more nor less than a beauty competition! Again an article in the *Marathon and Distance Runner* (April 1983), describing the woman's British Marathon team as 'The ladies of the Evian Squad . . .', went on to say 'the results were listed and last but not least they finished with . . . pretty Sally MacDairmid [who] proved that her marathon was no flash in the pan . . .'. Why should sports writers, above all, trivialise women athletes in this way? Unfortunately there are just too many examples, one final one perhaps being a pre-interview description of Mary Decker as having 'eye catching good looks, America's athletics darling'. No-one describes male athletes in this way.

Of course, if a top sportswoman isn't turned into a beauty star, her motherhood can always be emphasised. British runner Joyce Smith for instance, so often described as 'Supermum, mother of two', was as recently as October 1984 described in *Athletics Weekly* as 'Everybody's favourite mum'.

Female or not?

And if a sportswoman isn't belittled by being turned into a sex object or wife and mother, she can always be presented as unfeminine. One particular runner who constantly receives this sort of treatment is the Czechoslovakian runner Jarmila Kratochvilova. She is a fine and powerful runner who has broken the world 400m and 800m records. Apparently as a girl of twelve she 'was already able to toss a pitch fork of hay up into the loft as well as any adult farmer' (*Athletics Weekly*, 11 February 1984). The criticism, of course, is that she looks too masculine. She therefore receives appalling treatment from commentators such as Ron Pickering who, commentating on the 1983 World Championships, described her as 'not a very feminine young lady', typical of the sort of comment addressed to women who achieve world records without make-up.

Prejudice, perhaps, reached its height in a letter which appeared in the same issue of *Athletics Weekly*. Among other things the writer said:

> 'Jarmila Kratochvilova . . . makes a mockery of women's athletics and indeed makes me ponder the future direction of the sport. I suppose if women are to run faster, the more they can become male "clones", the stronger they will be in relation to their weaker sisters. . . . It is as if Donna Hartley, bless her, suddenly reappeared in athletics looking . . . like Bill [Donna's husband] . . . for me . . . there is no pleasure in watching races in which Kratochvilova is involved. There is a certain macabre fascination . . . like watching a buffalo running in a herd of gazelles . . .'

Such attitudes are only too common, we can't be athletes on our own terms; if we succeed it is because we are men, look like men, or run like men. The implication taken to its extreme is that we may not even be 'real' women at all! To prove a point we may even have to undergo a sex test (see page 63). This is precisely what the talented Jarmila has to carry with her – an IAAF femininity certificate!

Discrimination takes other forms too. In mixed races women face various kinds of put-down. Prizes, for instance, are frequently only half the value of the men's prizes. In a British 10-mile road race Caroline Rodgers was pleased to come in fourth but she certainly lost out on the prizes. While the first three men won sports kit, the first three women won: a bread bin (1st prize), a brush and comb (2nd prize) and a plastic hand bag (3rd prize). That was in 1979. But things have changed – the brush and comb set has now been replaced by small . . . hair dryers! The men's prizes, however, get bigger. The winner of the Wakefield Half Marathon on 9 September 1983 earned himself a trip to New Zealand, while the winner of the women's event won herself a mini-break in the Dutch Bulb

fields – well under half the value of the men's prize. In 1983 I myself did a fun run and came in first woman. I should have won a bottle of wine; the first man should have won a crate of wine. I stood my ground, however, complained against discrimination (ungrateful woman I heard them whisper) and the wine was shared. And, unfortunately, in Britain this pattern is repeated with prize money. This is not the case in the United States. The female and male winners of the 10km race in Las Vegas held in the autumn of 1984 each earned $500,000 (payments spread over fifty years).

As a British sportswoman in a mixed race, too, there is the constant risk of being ignored. For instance, magazine reports on a mixed race may refer to the first three women's places and times but other women runners in the race usually receive no mention. By contrast as many as the first fifty male runners may be mentioned. British media coverage of women's events is likewise negligible. During 1983 and 1984, while the men's World Cross Country Championships were shown in their entirety on British television, the women's event merited coverage of only about 2 to 4 minutes. As Jennifer Hargreaves has pointed out,

> [the] screening of women in action in . . . sports such as athletics . . . has, without doubt, increased their popularity, but Paul Doherty, Head of Sport at Granada Television, expressed the dominant status quo position when he declared that, in general, sports in which women participate do not attract viewers . . .

This in turn becomes a 'self-fulfilling prophecy': if women's events are not shown, they are hardly going to become popular.

Recent developments

Since about the mid-1970s, the question of sex discrimination in sport has become a major and international point of focus for athletes, sports bodies, feminists, sociologists and others. In Britain, for instance, the Sports Council has taken an important lead and is playing an active part, both in employing women in administrative positions and in concentrating on women in sport. It has set up a Working Party on Women in Sport to investigate reasons for the low participation of women in sport and recreation. It has also launched a policy of *Sport for All*, and has initiated among other things, Action Sport which has a high proportion of female leaders and was set up in September 1982 to encourage people within the Inner London communities who would not normally do so, to take up sport. At the same time, the Inner London Education Authority has produced a major report on sex discrimination in sport in British schools, and hopefully this will produce some positive changes.

Women and other groups within society face discrimination in sport on the ground of 'race, disability, or sexuality'. This is now being recognised and a number of groups have been set up to promote the interests of either women or other 'disadvantaged' persons in sport. Among such groups are the British Women's Sport

Federation (BWSF) set up in September 1984 which is similar to the San Francisco Women's Sport Foundation in the United States, the Foundation for Afro Asians in Sport (FAAS) which was set up in 1983, and the British Sports Association for the Disabled (BSAD). The needs at least are being recognised; what is required is more such groups.

Above all women themselves are pinpointing discrimination by participating in sport and demanding status. Projects such as Avon/Running 'Sister's Project' organised by Alison Turnbull and Geoffrey Cannon of the British *Running* magazine have had great success in getting women runners started in running, by matching novice women runners/joggers with more experienced women runners to help them build confidence and share problems. 141 women turned up at the Eastleigh Women and Running Seminar (creche available) organised by Chris Benning in 1984. This means women who run can meet together and discuss their problems and successes. While such events show that there is a need to help, encourage and educate women about running, they also show that women want to run and want to learn about running.

Another exciting development has been the 'Toronto Women Running'. As a club they have established contacts with women runners in all parts of Canada, to share common concerns and to promote women's running. A National Women's Running Conference was held which attracted women from Canada and the USA. From this the North American Network of Women Runners was set up in 1979. The network was established to 'promote women running in different ways', and various groups were formed to deal with the different problems that women face as runners such as organising a women's marathon in the Olympics to safety, exploitation, race, gayness, and so on.

International companies New Balance, Avon and Evian all sponsored women-only races in 1984. Nike in conjunction with the British magazine, *Women's Own*, also sponsored a 10km fun run in Britain in which 17,000 women participated, many of them novice runners. In September 1984 the Avon International Women's Marathon Championship was held in Paris, France. It was the culmination of a series of fifty women-only races held in 19 countries, and more than 1,000 women took part. In fact, overall, Avon International estimated that in 1984 some 60,000 women were running on their circuits in the nineteen countries where their products are sold.

It was only in 1976 that Dave Billington, husband of the runner Lyn Billington, organised the first all-women marathon in the United Kingdom – two laps around Heathrow airport. Twenty women participated, none of whom had trained properly, but even then three women achieved times under three hours. Christine Ready was the winner in 2 hours 50 minutes 55 seconds. Eight years later, in 1984, women runners were finally receiving some sort of recognition, but we still have a long way to run.

6 THE BARRIERS IN FRONT OF WOMEN

Running is the cheapest and easiest way into fitness, an absolute bargain. And yet, even today, there are far fewer women running than there are men. Most adult women do not run – why? Below we list what we think are the most common barriers:

But I don't know how to run

Gill is a runner now, but like Claudia and many other women, she hated sport at school because she wasn't any good at it. She entered the school cross country, but always came in last, so consequently didn't enjoy it. And, like so many girls today, she spent a lot of time trying to get out of sport. Adult women who never carry on any sport when they leave school often find they can't run, they have forgotten how to. Like anything else, it is a skill that has to be practised. When I first started to run as an adult, I did a 100m race, something that I used to do regularly at school. But, I found I couldn't run, I was all arms and legs and didn't know how to get to the end. Mary was also surprised to find that she couldn't run when she first tried to. Running is something that most of us don't continue with once we leave school. Therefore, even if women do want to try, they have no confidence, and feel that they can't.

Running is a perfectly natural activity. As the history section shows, however, in the past women have been discouraged or even prevented from taking part in sport generally, and some specific sports in particular, among them running. Today running does form a part of most school curricula although girls' events tend to be shorter or less strenuous than boys'. What does happen, however, is that for all sorts of reasons, girls drop out of sport while boys carry on. And if women do take up sport again, it is usually one of the so-called female sports activities such as gymnastics, yoga, keep fit, tennis or swimming. Until recently very few women would have thought of taking up running as a pastime. After all, how many well-known women runners can women model themselves on anyway? For boys or men there are plenty – from Roger Bannister, Chris Chataway, Emile Zatopek right through to Steve Ovett or Steve Cram. Whether successful or not, male athletes are popular and can be copied. But how many women have heard of Wendy Sly the 1984 Olympic 3,000m silver medallist, or Chris Benning who has written the foreword to this book and who came fifth in the 1984 Olympic 1500m? There are plenty of role models for women in tennis, horse riding or gymnastics but only too few in running.

Until recently also the woman who might have wanted to take up jogging or running was likely to be intimidated by the dominance of men in jogging or athletic clubs, or even by athletic women. Lacking in confidence anyway, novice women runners are often frightened that they won't be able to keep up the pace. Fortunately the jogging boom and highly-publicised events such as the New York, London or Melbourne Marathons are finally showing women that running is a possibility for them.

But it's so masculine

Gill remembers only too well as 'a fat eleven year old running for a bus, and my mother saying to me "Don't worry dear, ladies don't

"Don't worry, dear, ladies don't run..."

run" '. The fact is that vigorous activity such as running, because it makes you strong, makes you sweat, and because it requires exertion, has traditionally been regarded as 'unladylike', suitable for men but not for a 'real' woman!

Running goes directly against the anti-exercise conditioning that women receive from birth onwards. As women we learn very early on that sport is a male domain, that strenuous activity is inappropriate for women. In fact expectations start even before birth – an active, lively foetus is almost invariably seen as male – the he's-kicking-so-much-I-bet-he'll-be-a-footballer syndrome, while a quiet, passive foetus is automatically assumed to be a girl.

The same message continues once the child is born – girls and boys are treated differently. Elena Gianini Bellotti in her book *Little Girls* describes very clearly how girls are brought up to be passive, while many studies, including one carried out by Sussex University during the late 1970s, confirm the fact that there are real sex differences in the way most parents treat their children. Boys are encouraged to rush around, be aggressive and active, while girls are encouraged to be more passive and less boisterous, held back and actively discouraged from expressing themselves through active play. It's enough to make you rush immediately to the front door demanding your right to run.

Of course it isn't necessary to read these studies, you probably only have to think of your own upbringing, or that of other children. When my son Tom was a toddler, I took him to visit a friend who also had a toddler of much the same age, but a girl, Kelly. They were very similar in personality, both were very active, both liked a rough and tumble. They were having one of their boisterous fights, when an adult commented: 'You can see Tom's a real boy, but Kelly's a little bitch.' Her active behaviour was frowned on; but Tom's was accepted as 'natural'.

Running is active behaviour too; it's also natural. But active behaviour is rewarded and seen as natural for boys, not for girls. At the same time, in lots of subtle and not so subtle ways, girls are also being taught that they are the so-called 'weaker sex', and the twin images of frail femininity and sport as a male activity continue throughout school, perpetuated wittingly or not, by teachers themselves. Although the situation is changing and Janet now joins in with John and his ball game, rather than just being an onlooker, sex discrimination in school sport is still rampant. At junior level, cross-country races, for instance, are often shorter for girls than for boys. During the cross-country matches for nine to ten year olds held at one of our local schools, for example, the girls ran exactly half the distance set for boys. And girls are 'protected' in other ways too. On rainy, wet days in one of the schools where I worked, the boys were sent out on cross-country runs when the football pitch was unusable; the girls were sent to play netball in the playground. No question of getting muddy for them! In another local school, too, and again in bad weather, if girls are not actually kept indoors to do gym or dance, they are much more likely to be allowed to wear gloves, jumpers and track suits outside than boys. Boys, instead, are expected to struggle out in truly manly fashion, dressed only in their football kit. The messages are clear: girls are frail, fragile beings, boys are tough and aggressive, 'naturally' suited for sport and difficult conditions.

Even so, up to about the age of eleven, participation in most sports, other than say rugby or football, is still fairly acceptable for girls. After that age, however, and from puberty onwards, everything changes as the messages from schools, media, family and so on about what is considered appropriate for women get louder and louder. And one of the things traditionally not considered appropriate is sport. Most sports instructors, writers, and the Sports Council itself would agree that, from about the age of thirteen, girls drop out of sport in droves. The fact is that sport offers very little status or rewards for the teenage girl; she is much more likely to win approval from her friends if she has a boyfriend than if she wins an 800m race. Peer group pressure is very strong at this age and many teenage girls may be influenced by friends who don't like sport. The boyfriend's opinion too counts for a lot. You only have to look at magazines and comics aimed at teenage girls, particularly the 'true romance' sort of story to see just how inferior girls of this age may feel: taking just one example – boy walks into room saying 'Glad you're here. Sorry I'm late. Come on we're wasting time, let's go to the disco'; while she is thinking 'Can't think what he sees in me . . .'. If that is typical, it is unlikely that a girl is going to run unless she has the full approval of her boyfriend, particularly in the type of male-dominated society that we live in, where nearly all the rules are made by men, and where a woman's success in sport may even present a real threat to a man's masculinity.

Unlike teenage boys whose continuing sport involvement is seen as 'natural' and is rewarded by approval and respect from peers, adults and so on, the girl who continues in sport may face a great deal of role conflict because it does not conform with what is considered to be feminine. As a result the girl who is a good runner at school risks a lot when she trains hard to become better and is likely to be considered an overgrown 'tomboy'; in effect her sexuality is at risk. It is hardly surprising then that women are more likely to watch sport than to take part in it, or like the American cheerleaders, encourage men's achievements.

And if the situation is bad for Western women, it is far worse for Asian and Islamic women whose upbringing is far more repressive, bound by deeply ingrained cultural and religious views about women. While black women athletes have traditionally received considerable recognition, particularly in the United States, it is still not considered at all acceptable for an Asian woman to participate in sport on grounds of blasphemy. Even in Britain where there are large Asian communities it is likely that social and cultural considerations will still prevent the emergence of young female Asian athletes for many years to come.

Although it is true that women are running and winning events, we must look beautiful while we are doing it. Jarmila Kratochvilova, the Czechoslovakian runner, has broken the 400m and 800m world records, but rather than receiving applause for her abilities she was described as a 'not very feminine young lady' by a British sports commentator because she did it without make-up and with muscles. Does anyone label the slim Sebastian Coe, as a 'not very masculine young man'?

Simone de Beauvoir, the French feminist, has said that

> In effect it is not by increasing her human value that [a woman] will gain in a male's eyes, it is by modelling herself in accordance with masculine dreams . . . to be feminine is to reveal oneself as impotent, futile, and docile. . . .

I wonder what would happen if women suddenly decided to stop carrying the shopping, the children and the pushchair up and down flights of stairs, or on and off buses, on the grounds that it is far too strenuous for us, that it is making us too strong and much too masculine?

But everyone will see me

'We feel embarrassed about our bodies. . . . I hate taking my skirt off, I think everybody is looking at me.' That's how one fourteen year old girl describes her feelings about getting changed for sport at school. Another girl, the same age, explaining why she hates sport, says 'and then you have to run around in them horrible blue knickers . . . it's easier at this school because it's all girls, if it was a mixed school it would be even worse. . . .'. These are comments from just two girls, but there are a lot of other teenage girls who would say exactly the same thing. And not only young women, but older women too are enormously conscious of and embarrassed about their bodies, sure that they are too fat or too thin, far too self-conscious to take off their clothes, put on shorts and run where everyone can see them.

Really it would be surprising if we felt any different. Teenage comics, magazine articles, advertisements on television are all aimed at turning us into a stereotyped female, that stunningly attractive woman who stares you in the face every time you open a magazine. Images like this tell us all the time that we should look a certain way, wear that sort of make-up or this particular fashion. And of course, just as the Jane Fonda or Raquel Welch work-out books tell you, you must be slim; no fat thighs, no heavy breasts or thick waists are allowed; these are quite out.

Images such as these are powerful, and they are sold to women and young girls to copy. They have very little bearing on what women actually look like; instead they become a source of anxiety. If you follow this work-out schedule, you too can look like Jane Fonda or Raquel Welch in your forties. But most women never will; to achieve that sort of appearance, even if we could, takes time and money. While leotards, slimming diets, work-out and dance studios are making fat profits for a few, they are also succeeding in making ordinary women overconscious about the way they look, because underlying the image is the message that if you look like this, you will be attractive to men.

That message gets through very early. Unfortunately it is not only the images we see that affect us, but comments that we as women receive, particularly from men. Ann's daughter, Sarah, is only six years old but already she won't do gym in knickers any more because the boys in her class make fun of her. The teenage years are the worst. It is at this time that a young girl's body goes through major changes; periods start, breasts develop and so on. It is a particularly awkward and self-conscious time, not helped by experiences at school, for instance, catcalls, jeers from boys and 'horrible blue knickers' for sport. Hardly an incentive to take up running or any other outdoor sport. Experiences such as these can last a lifetime, particularly if your appearance doesn't match up to the 'ideal'. One of our friends, Julie, now in her thirties, still won't do any outdoor sport because when she was at school she felt 'big and clumsy', and still thinks that her thighs are too large.

Women are still frightened to be seen doing something that is supposedly a male activity, and many suffer that well-known feeling of being looked at and criticised. Running is an outdoor activity; it does mean taking off some clothes, so that any feelings of inadequacy you have about yourself are made worse. Most of the women interviewed for this book would never have started running if they had not seen other women do it. In 1982, for our Woman's Day of Sport (see page 118), we handed out questionnaires to get some feedback from the women who came. Many of them commented that before that day they had had 'a neurosis about things like bad acne, hairiness or ugliness in general . . .'. For those women the all-woman Day provided enormous encouragement. But they were just a few. A comment from a Canadian woman at Chris Benning's running seminar is probably more typical: when asked what she would like to see in running she replied: 'More British women running in the parks and on the streets. Where are they? I never see any.' It's hardly surprising.

But I haven't got the time

Jane doesn't run because she says she just hasn't got the time. She's got two children, a husband and a part-time job. As she says,

> 'it's non-stop in the morning. There's the baby and Sarah to feed, my husband to get to work. Then I've got to get the kids to the childminder, get myself to work. After work it's pick up the kids, back home, make supper so there's something ready when my husband gets home, put the kids to bed, and that's just about my day. . . .'

Most of the women that participate in sport are middle class; working-class women have traditionally had neither the time nor the leisure to participate in sport.

When we asked a thirteen year old girl whether she would continue with sport once she left school, she replied 'but when I have children I won't have time. . . .' She was assuming two things: firstly, that she would automatically have children, and secondly, that sport would not be important enough to make time for. Most young women automatically assume that once they reach adulthood their time is going to be taken up by childrearing and domestic chores, maybe a waged job, but not by sport.

As we've already explained, sport is seen as a male activity anyway, so it's not surprising that many women are going to think that it is fairly irrelevant to their lives. We often don't see sport as an available or 'natural' option in the way that men do. But it is also more than that. Whether as wives and mothers or not, we do make time for others but not for ourselves, perhaps because we don't see our lives as very important anyway. Our heads are always crammed with the needs of others; we even live our lives through others – my husband, my children, my boyfriend. Often, too, we don't assume our right just to go out of the door, in the same way that a man can whether he is going to football, out to work, or to the pub. Instead we have to arrange babysitters if we want to go out, or have to ask 'permission'. Lynn, for instance, has occasionally thought about running, just to see what it is like. Her husband wouldn't mind at all if she did, particularly as he runs himself. But Lynn feels he has one big advantage, that he can just walk out of the door and go for a run, while she feels that she has to ask him if he would mind looking after the children when she goes out. As a result, she has never tried running, instead she goes swimming together with the whole family.

Whether it is in our minds, whether we actually stop ourselves, or whether someone deliberately stops us, the fact is that we not only have to 'uncondition' ourselves to find time for ourselves but also we have to fight for the right to do it.

So why the barriers?

For eleven year old Sophie the reason is that as women 'we're not judged equally . . . and *that* all started because Eve was doing the wrong thing'. Sophie doesn't believe in Adam and Eve and neither do I, but according to the Bible, it was Adam who told tales to God that Eve had given him the forbidden fruit, a 'wrong doing' that we, as all subsequent Eves, have been paying for ever since. God punished Adam by ordering him to 'eat the herb of the field' – not a bad punishment for doing something wrong, after all Adam didn't *have* to eat the apple! Eve's punishment was much more oppressive. Firstly, she was 'in sorrow [to] bring forth children'; secondly, and more significantly, she was told 'and thy desire shall be to thy husband and he shall rule over thee. . . .'. Truly unfair, but two duties that have shaped most women's lives ever since.

From biblical times onwards, in Western societies anyway, men have dominated women, and Eve's experience has been repeated time and time again. For instance, and as we have already mentioned, the Victorian ideal of womanhood was that of beauty, passivity, subordination to husband, and of self-restraint. Escape into sport or almost any other area outside the home was therefore quite unthinkable, an attitude writ loud and clear by Pierre de Coubertin in 1935 when he stated that the only role of women in the Olympic games should be that of crowning the (male) victor. Unfortunately these attitudes are still very much with us; they form an essential part of the patriarchal society we live in. By patriarchal society we mean a society in which men have power over women. In social terms it *is* a man's world. The majority of politicians, police, judges, directors and sports administrators are men. Women constitute half the world's population, perform nearly two-thirds of its work hours, receive one-tenth of the world's income and own less than one-hundredth of the world's property. In a world where men hold actual power over women, it is hardly surprising that at every level our actions (as women) are geared to what we are told or what we think men expect of us. From cradle to the grave the decisions we make, the way we behave, the very clothes we wear and the body images we aspire to, are modelled on and reflect the influence of a male-dominated society.

It is not surprising then that these barriers exist for women. Whether it is in our minds as a result of conditioning, or whether there actually is somebody who physically stops us, the barriers do exist. It might sound a bit drastic but for most women it has been and still is a fight for the right to run. What is so exciting is that, every day, more women are running through, or overcoming, these barriers.

7 THE WEAKER SEX? EXPLODING THE MYTHS

For centuries, women's non-involvement in sport has rested on the assumption that women are weaker than men, frail, delicate beings who for their own sakes should be protected and kept out of sport. Even today large numbers of people – women and men – hang onto the belief that women are the 'weaker sex'. Such beliefs are based on a number of long-standing myths about the nature of women and 'femininity'. Far from containing any truth these myths only reflect anti-woman prejudice. The longer these beliefs are held, however, the fewer will be the opportunities for women in sport, and the less likely women themselves are to take up running, or any other sport for that matter.

Having looked at the available evidence, we now want to challenge and dispel some of these myths once and for all, and to demonstrate that there are no physiological reasons to prevent women from running, or from achieving success through running.

Sport is counter-reproductive: you can't be a mother and an athlete too

Some of the most pernicious myths have to do with a woman's reproductive functions – with menstruation, pregnancy and childbirth. Put briefly, the argument goes that sport is damaging to a woman's reproductive process. Turned around, it is also argued that women, because of their reproductive functions, will never make top athletes. Heads you don't win, tails you lose! The question is, just how much truth is there in the following statements?

THAT RUNNING CAUSES MISCARRIAGES In 1962 a study of 800 athletic and non-athletic women was carried out by a Hungarian, Dr Gyula Erdelyi. It showed that, because of their greater fitness, the athletic women experienced far fewer complications in pregnancy, labour and childbirth than the non-athletic women. They had fewer miscarriages, less incidence of toxaemia (a serious condition that can occur in late pregnancy), and only half the need for caesarian deliveries than the non-athletes. Labour also was faster and less complicated, and delivery much easier for the athletes. The conclusion was quite clear – being an athlete makes childbirth easier.

Nor does running before or during pregnancy cause any harm to the unborn child. The great Dutch athlete, Fanny Blankers-Koehn, and more recently, the Norwegian marathon runner, Ingrid Kristiansen, are just two examples of women who competed during their pregnancies, and then went on to produce perfectly healthy children.

Finally, neither pregnancy nor childbirth have any adverse affect on a woman's sporting abilities. This myth should have died years ago. All evidence shows that, during the first three months of pregnancy anyway, there is no apparent decline in a woman's sporting performance. As far back as 1948 Fanny Blankers-Koehn won four Olympic gold medals for athletics while she was pregnant and, as a mother, went on to set further world records. Mary Rand and the Polish Irena Szewinska are two other outstanding athletes who have gained Olympic medals after producing children. In the 1956 Olympics, ten of the twenty Russian medal winners were pregnant when they earned their medals! More recently, Ingrid Kristiansen took part in the 1983 World cross-country championships, quite unaware of the fact that she was pregnant. Following the birth of her child she went on to complete the London Marathon in near world record time. All quite enough evidence to show that women's sporting achievements are not impaired by their reproductive functions. In fact, one German study has shown that women who returned to athletics after having children actually showed an increase in strength, endurance, and determination.

So pregnancy and childbearing do not affect women's athletic abilities, and running does not harm a woman's reproductive functions. Some women continue running throughout pregnancy to within days or even hours of labour; others, because of discomfort, prefer to switch to another form of exercise such as swimming. The decision is personal. If there is any doubt, check with a doctor, but provided there are no medical contraindications, the active woman can continue to run and compete during pregnancy without anxiety. Women who have had previous miscarriages, however, should reduce their running during the first three months of pregnancy, nor is it advisable to start running for the first time during pregnancy. Marathon running may possibly have adverse affects on the foetus if continued until late pregnancy, although this is not proved; more strenuous forms of training such as heavy, resistance work should be avoided. Running can be resumed fairly quickly after childbirth, subject to medical considerations; most runners start again in six weeks.

Incidentally, running does not affect breast-feeding either – it certainly does not inhibit the flow of milk unless you get over-tired. The more relaxed you are, and the better you feel, the easier breast-feeding is.

THAT RUNNING CAUSES MENSTRUAL PROBLEMS

There is no reason at all why women should not run at all stages of their menstrual cycle. Many women runners say that, far from causing problems, running helps to regulate periods, and to ease pain. This is borne out by studies carried out in the mid-1970s which confirmed that running, or any regular exercise, can lead to a reduction in painful periods (dysmenorrhoea), headaches, and general discomfort. In fact these studies seem to show that irregular, painful periods are much less common among fit, athletic women than among non-active women. Sustained, intensive training, particularly for middle- or long-distance events can cause reduced periods (oligomenorrhoea) or even loss of periods (amenorrhoea). The exact reasons are not known. Whatever the reason, there is no evidence to suggest that this is harmful. Normal menstruation always returns when exercise is reduced, and fertility is unaffected. In a study of female long-distance runners published in 1975, only 19 per cent had very irregular periods, and 23 per cent had no periods at all for months at a time. Four of those whose periods stopped have since produced healthy children; one of them has actually had four children. Just as a matter of interest, many ballerinas suffer from amenorrhoea, but no-one ever suggests that women shouldn't do ballet!

Conversely, menstruation is not a handicap to achievements in running. Obviously periods affect individual women in different ways, but records have been set and gold medals won by women during menstruation as at any other time. During the 1976 Olympics, for instance, an American swimmer won three gold medals and broke a world record while at the height of her period. In a study published in 1965 on women athletes at the Tokyo Olympics, 37 per cent of women said their performances were quite unaffected by periods; 28 per cent said the effects varied; and only 19 per cent said that the effect was 'always bad'. The fact is that a woman's ability as a runner is not affected by periods any more than it is by any other factor.

Women do suffer one physical disadvantage in relation to men, and probably only one – they have 15 per cent less haemoglobin (the red oxygen-carrying pigment in the blood) than men. This has nothing to do with menstrual flow, but with the male's greater production of the hormone testosterone. Anaemia is a potential problem for women athletes, some of whom are known to be up to 25 per cent deficient in stored iron, an important element in the production of haemoglobin. Extra iron, either in the diet or as a supplement, might be necessary.

THAT STRENUOUS EXERCISE DAMAGES A WOMAN'S REPRODUCTIVE ORGANS This myth is usually given as justification for keeping women out of pole-vaulting, namely that falling from a height might jar or dislodge a woman's internal organs. Recently the myth has been updated; one of the latest rumours is that jogging causes prolapse of the womb. There's no evidence for either argument. Prolapse is usually caused by damage during childbirth. In addition, a woman's reproductive organs – uterus, fallopian tubes, ovaries – are remarkably well protected deep inside the body. They are shock resistant as well: the body acts as a shock absorber so that any force reaching the uterus is greatly lessened. Male genitals are far more vulnerable but no-one suggests keeping men out of sport. The double standard again, underlined by the fact that pole-vaulting itself, as Dr Elizabeth Ferris has pointed out, is mechanically-speaking a composite of other sports – running, gymnastics, and high jump – events from which women are not excluded.

Although it has little to do with running, there is a story which illustrates just how ludicrous these myths of female frailty can be. In 1978, eight women joined an American expedition to Annapurna in the Himalayas. The leaders of the expedition were men, and they were very worried about the women's ability to cope with the stress of altitude and frostbite. They needn't have been so anxious. Seven out of the eight women reached the summit with no altitude sickness at all, and not one of them suffered frostbite. Five of the men, however, did suffer frostbite – on their testicles!

THAT RUNNING DAMAGES A WOMAN'S BREASTS A two-year study of US high-school girls taking part in badminton, basketball, gymnastics, cross-country running, netball, swimming, tennis, volleyball, and track and field athletics, found that not one single breast injury was reported during that time. Breast injuries are among the rarest of all injuries seen in athletics, and there is no evidence to link them with running. When breast injuries do occur, anyway, they are mostly in the form of minor bruising. And, to scotch another myth, severe bruising does

not lead to cancer (an argument often put up to prevent women from taking part in rugby or boxing).

In fact women cannot be kept out of sport on the grounds of being more injury prone than men. Injuries to either sex usually occur because of carelessness, inadequate training, unfitness and so on. Where these are taken care of, injury rates are much the same for both sexes. And if there really is a genuine risk of injury, as in say rugby or boxing, there is no reason why women shouldn't wear protective clothing as men do. If a sport is too dangerous for women, it is too dangerous for men. But the double standard continues to operate: and despite evidence to the contrary, women are still excluded from certain sports for 'their own good', whether they like it or not. Which leads us on to the issue of women's capabilities:

Anything we can do, they can do better – or can they?

The most repressive myths are those that have ignored or denied women's capabilities. All of them are variations on a single theme – that men are physically stronger and more capable than women. As sport is defined in male terms of speed, strength, and power, these myths have 'justified' and perpetuated discrimination against women in sport: even more, they have, in the past, been accepted by large numbers of women themselves, making them feel like inadequate intruders in a man's world. The assumptions run deep. After all, the most effective way of dismissing an athlete's capabilities has traditionally been to describe that athlete as running, throwing or jumping 'like a girl'. What we want to do now is to find out just how much truth there is in the following assumptions.

WOMEN ARE THE WEAKER SEX This is really the pivot on which all other myths turn, namely the belief that men are stronger than women and that only men have the necessary and 'natural' abilities for sport. Certainly the average man is generally taller, stronger and heavier than the average woman. The average man too has more muscle mass, a larger heart, and a greater lung capacity than the average woman. There are therefore significant differences between women and men. But while they might be grounds for segregating women and men in certain sports – just as featherweight and heavyweight boxers do not compete against each other – it doesn't follow that women should be denied the same opportunities. Nor does it indicate anything about performance *potential* in women.

What recent evidence is demonstrating quite conclusively is that differences *within* a sex are actually greater than differences *between* the sexes, and that physical fitness and training are far more influential than gender. Differences in muscular strength have traditionally been used to prove male superiority. At physical maturity, men are on average about 10 per cent larger and their muscle mass about double that of a woman. But studies carried out by Dr J. Wilmore and others during the 1970s showed that these differences are more pronounced in the arms and shoulders than in the lower body. In fact, leg strength relative to body size is almost identical in both sexes; when expressed relative to body mass, women are actually stronger in the thighs than men. It was also found that with progressive weight training, women can quite substantially increase their muscular strength. During a ten-week training programme a group of young, non-athletic women improved their strength by 30-50 per cent. Incidently, to explode another myth: this did not 'masculinise' the women. Weight training does not produce bulging s/he-wo/men. Muscle bulk depends on the presence of specific hormones – androgens – in the body, most particularly testosterone which is produced to a greater extent in males. And even male weight trainers may require supplementary hormones to produce the required muscle effect.

Interestingly, until puberty there is very little difference between boys and girls in terms of size, strength or reaction times. In fact girls of nine to twelve are often larger and stronger than boys of the same age because they mature earlier. From puberty onwards, the advantage among untrained adolescents swings decidedly in favour of boys. The reasons are largely hormonal, androgens being responsible for the denser muscle mass and larger bones typical of men, but are also social and cultural. It is simply that young women are not encouraged to develop their physical potential in the same way as men, but tend to follow more sedentary lives.

It has also been argued that women do not have the same potential as men because, having smaller lungs and hearts, and less haemoglobin and muscle mass, we do not have the same capacity to take in and use up oxygen, a crucial element in performance potential. The average woman apparently pumps 16 per cent or so less blood than a man, and uses some 15-25 per cent less oxygen during exertion. And it has been argued that a woman's aerobic capacity is only 70-75 per cent of that of a man. But these figures refer to sedentary women. With training these gaps disappear and it has been found that highly trained female athletes are 25 per cent more efficient in physical work capacity than untrained men. Highly trained male athletes still have a greater work capacity than trained women, but where oxygen uptake is related to lean body mass rather than to total body weight, this difference is minimal. So, in the end, it is training rather than gender which is critical. It is not relevant to compare untrained men and women; it is certainly wrong to exclude women from sports on the grounds that their potential is less, or even to assume that women will never catch up men. Perhaps more relevant is to ask whether women actually want to compete with men?

THAT RUNNING 'IS A LITTLE TOO STRENUOUS FOR WOMEN'

This is what the International Olympic Committee said in 1978 about women's participation in the 3,000m. Until very recently it was assumed that women just did not have the necessary stamina for high-level endurance events. Individual achievements, such as Gertrude Ederle's setting the English cross-Channel swimming record in 1937, were regarded as freakish and untypical. Today, however, women themselves are going out and challenging this sort of assumption by their participation in long-distance running and other events.

Women today are running regularly over the mile, 1500m and 3,000m. They are also competing in longer road races and track events – from 5,000m and 10,000m (not in the Olympics) up to the marathon and beyond. And what is more, they are not only catching up with men but in some events may actually have more potential. As might be expected, unlike men, information on women runners is still sparse, but even so, various facts are emerging that suggest that women are probably better suited than men to endurance events.

The average female has a higher percentage of body fat than the average male, a fact that was believed to limit women's sporting potential. In fact this extra fat gives women more ability to withstand fatigue, and it is more readily burned as fuel than in men. So when male marathon runners burn up their bodies' supplies of glycogen after about two hours running, and they 'hit the wall', women burn their body fat more efficiently, conserving their glycogen reserves, and don't suffer in the same way. The myth has always been that this extra body fat is a 'natural' disadvantage for women – but now it seems that the reverse is true.

It is also being argued that women regulate their body temperature better than men. Again, because women do not sweat as much as men, and sweating is a form of heat control, it had been assumed that women are more vulnerable than men to heat stress. Again this myth can go. Women marathon runners in fact exhibit far less heat stress or fluid loss symptoms than men, probably because, according to Dr Weinham of the University of Illinois and Dr Christine Wells of Arizona State University, women regulate their body temperature more efficiently. The argument is that men sweat 'wastefully'; that women, because they lose less sweat, are less at risk from fluid loss. It is also argued that the female sex hormone, estrogen, may encourage the formation of blood vessels, so that more blood can be conducted to the skin surface for cooling.

Similar findings are occurring in other areas too, namely long-distance swimming and cycling. Although evidence is sparse, no doubt because of the lack of attention paid to the fewer women involved, it certainly looks as if women's potential has been considerably underestimated or completely ignored for years, and that it is far greater than has ever been assumed. What have been presented as 'natural' disadvantages turn out to be inherent advantages, and endurance events, far from being too strenuous for women, may be a 'little too strenuous' for men!

THAT WOMEN WILL NEVER BE AS 'GOOD' AS MEN

Arguments over whether women athletes can ever be as 'good' as or equal to men still rage. In fact all the evidence shows that women are catching up fast, and perhaps nowhere more obviously than in running. In 1928 the women's 800m record set by Lina Radke of Germany was 25 seconds slower than that of the men; by 1980 when Nadezhda Olizarenka of the Soviet Union set a new record, the gap had closed to 8 seconds. Marathon achievements have been even more remarkable. In 1976 Jacqueline Hansen of the United States became the first woman to complete the marathon in under 2 hours 40 minutes. At that time the gap between the men's and women's best times was more than 28 minutes. Only seven years later, in 1983, the gender gap had shrunk by half to 14 minutes. But during that same seven-year period men had shaved only 1 minute 42 seconds off their time. And there is no reason at all to assume that this gender gap should not continue to narrow. Dr Kenneth Dyer of Adelaide University, in his book *Catching up the Men*, has predicted that in marathon running, women may well have caught up with men by the end of the 1980s; that in the 3,000m they may be running as fast as men by 2003; and in the 400m by the year 2020. The facts therefore quite clearly explode the myth.

But can you be an athlete and a woman too?

We have shown that there are no physiological reasons whatsoever why women should not take part in any sport. But one more myth – perhaps the most insidious – needs to be shattered. The argument that a woman whose sporting achievements are as good as a man's may not biologically be a woman. A smear often directed at, say, East European athletes such as Jarmila Kratochvilova.

This attitude is epitomised by the sex test, probably one of the most punitive and humiliating forms of sex discrimination ever. The test was originally instituted in the 1960s apparently to make sure that men were not entering women's events and, according to the medical code of the IOC, is aimed at ensuring that 'competitors in sports restricted to women must comply with prescribed tests for femininity'. It is based on a rigid biological definition of male and female, namely chromosome configuration. In women, normal chromosome configuration is XX, in men XY. Cells are taken from either the mouth or perhaps a strand of hair, and tested for the presence of Y chromosomes, which would result in the automatic disqualification from competition. Only female athletes are tested.

The test takes no account of chomosomal abnormalities that do occur. For instance, there are quite 'normal' men who possess an extra X chromosome – the so-called Klinefelters syndrome. Again there are perfectly 'normal' women with Turner's syndrome who possess XO chromosomes. Likewise, women may have non-functioning ovaries and also fail the sex test. In fact the list of possible abnormalities and exceptions is very long, and it is now doubtful whether it is possible to arrive at a fixed definition of maleness and femaleness.

Sex testing was introduced because some female athletes displayed body shapes and abilities not considered to be stereotypically 'feminine'. It does not prove that sportswomen are not women, instead it demonstrates that our cultural stereotypes run deep, and that a woman's participation in sport is expected to conform to male expectations, values, standards and achievements. The sex test is as outdated, discriminatory and damaging as any of the previous myths and should, together with all the others, be thrown out once and for all.

As the evidence shows, there are no physiological or other reasons for excluding women from any sport; nor are there any reasons for assuming that women do not have the same potential as men, or that they may not, one day, equal or even surpass men.

What is encouraging is that women are discovering this for themselves, that they are going out and challenging the old stereotyped and repressive thinking about women's bodies and physical potential. Hopefully, in the not too distant future, these outdated myths will finally be rejected by men as well.

8 GETTING STARTED

You can lead a horse to water but you can't make it drink

The human body is designed for running, but for most women getting started is a real problem. First we have to set aside a time for ourselves without feeling guilty, and second we have to get out of the front door and do it. This means that all the anti-exercise conditioning that has gone on since birth, the feelings of being watched and judged, the myths that running might be bad for you, or unfeminine, must be forgotten. And, as sport is a male domain, we also have to overcome the fact that from birth few of us have been encouraged to do any sport unless we are 'good' at it. These problems are rarely taken seriously. Most books on running are written by men who automatically assume that a women will find it easy to get out of the front door. Books and articles describe clothing, techniques, fitness and so on in considerable detail, but the real problems for women of overcoming deeply-ingrained conditioning, of breaking life-long behaviour patterns, and of challenging our self-images are usually ignored.

For most women, getting out of that front door for the first time, in running gear, all ready to go, is really hard. We feel exposed, vulnerable, self-conscious, certain that everybody is watching us; getting out of that door means starting something directly opposed to our conditioning. Unfortunately, there is no magic formula for overcoming these barriers; like giving up smoking, starting to run requires a lot of determination, but once started, the rewards, feeling of achievement and increasing confidence, will more than compensate for the initial difficulties.

Think positive – it's all in the mind – or is it?

To start running we, as women, have to overcome various negative attitudes and objections either that we hold about ourselves, or that others have about us. To overcome them, we have to begin thinking positively about ourselves and our capabilities. Talking to other women, I think the most common objections to overcome are:

'BUT I DON'T KNOW HOW TO RUN' – the fear that we won't be any good at it. How often have you stopped yourself from doing something for just this reason? In fact running is a natural activity and one for which the human body is perfectly designed. There isn't any 'good' or 'bad' running, at this stage there's just running. You don't have to be 'good' at it. Ultimately you may want to set your own standards, but to start with, it's just a matter of running anyway you know how, and enjoying it. The finer points come later.

'BUT IT'S SO MASCULINE' – the idea that running is in some way 'unfeminine'. It's not. Girls run from a very early age – just look at any three year old – and it's an activity that women do very well as all the fun-runs, road races and marathons of the last few years demonstrate very clearly. The problem is that, traditionally, sport is a male activity and we feel insecure and uncertain of ourselves if we participate. Again it is a matter of being positive, of challenging what is stereotyped female in ourselves. To run we have to sweat, to exert ourselves, perhaps to go through some pain, and we have to forget all about our appearance and our conditioning. These things may not come easily, but they are worth it. Running is your right, and the feeling of confidence you gain from building up mileage will do more than anything else to make you sure of yourself and of what you are doing.

'BUT EVERYONE WILL SEE ME' – self-consciousness, worrying that people will see us and comment. Yes, people will see you, and they will make comments. These can range from something quite simple like 'Knees up' to something downright rude like 'You knackered cow'. And it can be daunting – it could even be described as verbal rape! Even as non-runners we are so often the target for catcalls, whistles, public comments about our appearance, body shape and so on, that it is sometimes a wonder that any woman even walks down the street with confidence, let alone runs.

Again, however, running brings its own confidence. Claudia, for instance, finds that 'running is such a wholesome thing to do, and makes you feel so liberated that when some bloke shouts, you begin to realise how ridiculous the whole thing is; that what you look like, the state of your hair, or lack of make-up are matters of total unconcern'.

In fact, the more you run, the less you will be concerned about your appearance because running makes you feel so good. I often think anyway, that women runners get these comments because we make the non-active person feel guilty, something that especially bothers the non-active male!

There are specific ways of dealing with comments and catcalls, and you'll probably find your own. One obvious strategy is just to ignore them, pretend they've not happened. Alternatively, and particularly where children are involved, I find it works to try to encourage the shouting onlookers to run with you. One comment that runners often get is 'I wish I had your energy', to which one running friend of mine replies 'So do I'.

Not all comments are unfriendly; some are encouraging. One of my friends, Kathleen, found that when she started running her neighbours quite obviously thought she was mad and chose to ignore her completely; now, however, they have got used to her running and greet her with encouraging waves and nods. The weather too seems to affect people's reactions. If it is fine, people seem much more tolerant; when you run in cold, wet weather, most people are likely to regard you with some suspicion. I was stopped in Hastings one rainy day by a motor-cyclist who asked me who I was because he thought he already knew all the mad people in the town! And, of course, there will always be the onlookers who ask you why you do it, to which, the more you run, the more you will provide the appropriate answer.

Yes, people will notice you running, but it isn't as bad today as it was say ten years ago when women runners were still fairly rare. And the more women run, the more women runners will be taken for granted and the fewer comments they will cause. And, in the end, just how seriously can you take a pot-bellied man who stands, cigarette in mouth watching you run by with the comment 'that's no good for you; it'll kill you'?

'BUT I HAVEN'T GOT TIME TO RUN' – our

reluctance to make time to run. As women it is easy for us to feel guilty about making time for ourselves. We don't like to leave the chores undone, or the children with someone else. Our time is limited by work and home commitments, but we are also conditioned to dedicate ourselves to others – to husbands, lovers, children – to make time and to be responsible for everyone around us but not for ourselves. In fact, a woman's very identity is too often defined in terms of others and, even more significantly, in terms of whether we are 'good' in the roles we take on – those of wives, sweethearts, mothers and career women. We rarely get the opportunity to be ourselves, or to please ourselves, and we feel guilty if we do so, even for a short while.

Guilt apart, lack of time can become an excuse in itself – running

does involve some self-discipline and, to start with, some slight discomfort. It's easy to push it to one side in favour of something less demanding. But, as Claudia and other women runners have said, making time for running is probably one of the biggest investments you can make. Running provides us with time; it gives us the opportunity to enjoy our thoughts; no-one is with us making demands or asking for our services; it is our time to unclog our minds from all worries and responsibilities. It provides a freedom and solitude that we, as women, have earned and that we owe to ourselves.

Before you start: safety checks

There really isn't any limit on who can run; most women if they are in reasonable physical condition can jog, no matter what their age. Mary started running when she was fifty-nine, Kathleen at the age of forty-four, Claudia when she was thirty-eight, and I was twenty-nine. Even so, it is wise to start off gently and if you've done no exercise for a long time, it is advisable to follow certain precautions.

CHECK WITH A DOCTOR IF:

1 you are over thirty-five;
2 you are a heavy smoker;
3 you are seriously overweight;
4 you are on prescribed medication;
5 you have any medical problems such as asthma, diabetes, heart conditions or high blood pressure;
6 you had rheumatic fever as a child;
7 you are troubled by pains in the joints, severe back pain, or arthritis;
8 you are worried that exercise may adversely affect your health.

YOU SHOULD NOT RUN IF:

1 you are recovering from illness or an operation;
2 you are pregnant, and have never run before. Many women athletes, such as the Norwegian middle- and long-distance runner Ingrid Kristiansen, have competed and won medals when pregnant, but they were already established runners. For the novice, it is not advisable to start running during pregnancy, instead it is better to wait until after the birth of your child;
3 you have a higher temperature than normal, perhaps because of a cold, virus infection and so on. These conditions will put an extra strain on your body, so be patient and wait until you feel better before starting your running;
4 you are injured. You must not run if you have an injury such as a strain or broken bones. Wait until everything has healed completely; if you start too soon you will find that the injury takes longer to heal.

Finally, Dr Joan Ullyot, the American physician and marathon runner, writes in her book *Women's Running*:

If you are under forty, or older but reasonably fit and active
(for instance if you hike, play tennis, swim or bike regularly)
you undoubtedly will get medical clearance. The mild to
moderate stress imposed on the heart during jogging actually
is less than that involved in more strenuous but intermittent
sports like tennis. So if you already know your heart is up to
the challenge, there is no need to check it out further.

And just to set the record straight a jog is only a slow run.

Starting off

When Mary started running she was surprised to find that it wasn't
quite as easy as she had imagined; in fact she found it difficult and
could only run for 2 minutes before collapsing, exhausted, against a
tree. Claudia, on her first run, managed a quarter-mile track and
then flopped with her head between her knees. I couldn't even run
for half a mile while Val had to make twenty attempts before she
could run three-quarters of a mile without discomfort. Many other
women have experienced exactly the same thing. However, over a
period of time, we have all built up our mileage from absolutely
nothing to as much as 10 or even 26 miles.

The first rule is – don't start off too fast; take it easy. Jogging is
just a little bit faster than walking, you should aim at a gentle pace
so that you can breathe normally, and even talk at the same time.
When you start running, your body is usually unfit and it is easy to
do too much too soon, and then to suffer for it. In fact it is
interesting to check your resting pulse rate (see page 92) before you
start your running, and then, some weeks or months later, to check
it again as a measure of your increasing fitness. All being well you
should find that your normal pulse rate becomes slower, a sign of
fitness. For safety, warm up by walking for 5 or 10 minutes before
running or jogging. Better still, do some stretching exercises (see
page 106).

When you get out for the first time, wear a watch and judge your
run by the amount of time you are out rather than by the actual
mileage. Aim to be out for 5 minutes on the first occasion. If you
find that you can't run for the entire time but have to walk part of
the way, that's perfectly alright. Next time you will find that you
will walk a little less, run a little more, and gradually you will find
yourself jogging for 10 minutes or so. Some women are quite
surprised by just how far they can run – like Chris, for instance,
who ran 2 miles on her first run; others find it much harder. But
even if it is hard, don't give up – you will make it. And the most

important thing is that you will be so proud of yourself.

Your sense of achievement alone will probably make you want to run again, so aim to go out again for those few minutes either every day, or every other day (see schedule on page 82). Your muscles will probably ache at first because you are using muscles that have not had to work before. And if you do feel very stiff, then wait until it wears off before trying again, although you may find that a gentle jog will itself ease the stiffness. At the end of your run, warm down with the stretching exercises on page 106. If you warm down, you are less likely to feel stiff.

Although the amount of time you run for is more important than the miles you do, most of us like a goal; we like to come back and say 'I've just run a mile or two'. When I first started, I set my own goal of running about 2¼ miles down to the bottom of the park and back again. It used to take me about 20 to 25 minutes depending on how I felt. And about a month after I had started, I entered my first cross-country race at Haywards Heath, Sussex (there were no fun runs in those days). The course itself covered 2 miles and I ran it at a steady pace in 17 minutes; I was so thrilled to have covered the entire course without stopping. I still think that first race was my best; I was so pleased with my achievement I actually glowed!

Just relax

Relaxation is the keynote to easy, comfortable running; embarrass-ment or tension are the chief obstacles. So many women when they start running look as if they are tied in knots just because they feel embarrassed and tense. The best way to overcome this is to run with a friend until you feel comfortable about running, and then to try it on your own. I had a very peculiar style when I first started – and used to flick my right leg outwards to the side, perhaps something to do with hurdling as a teenager. With practice, however, I overcame this awkwardness. The more you run, the more relaxed your style will be, and the more your body will adapt.

Run as smoothly as possible; try not to bounce. Your body should be relaxed but upright, shoulders down, head up, arms and hands at about waist level and bent at the elbow. Move loosely but smoothly – the most comfortable way to run is almost flat-footed, or heel first. Don't run on your toes or on the ball of your foot as this puts too much strain on the muscles and tendons in your legs and feet. Keep your arms low. And don't pump your arms, it's too tiring, just let them swing backwards and forwards in a relaxed, natural fashion. It is only when you go up hills that you may find a pumping action helps to 'pull' you up. Keep your hands loose but not floppy, and best way perhaps is to keep your hands lightly clenched but not squeezed tight.

Breathe correctly – this means breathing from your abdomen rather than from your chest. When you breathe in, your stomach should expand and it should flatten when you breath out. You can practise this sitting in a chair or lying on the floor, and then work on your breathing when you run. It is important to get this right because running itself makes you breathe hard and deeply, and incorrect breathing often causes a very painful side 'stitch' which itself is just spasm of the diaphragm, often caused by bad breathing. However, breathing does become easier the more relaxed you become about running; in fact it becomes part of the rhythm of running. I find that breathing through the mouth is easiest, although this depends on the individual runner, because apart from catching flies it's the most efficient way of breathing in more air.

Breathing will be harder when you run up hills because your body has to work harder. The town I live in – Hastings – is not the easiest place to run over any real distance because it is a mass of hills. Initially you will look at a hill and think 'Oh no, I can't do that' but if you do, then running up hills will become, and remain, a problem. The tip is not to look at what is coming, not to look at the top of the hill; instead look down and a little in front, lean slightly forward, and using your arms in a backwards and forward movement, shorten your stride until you reach the top. The first time you try a hill you might have to stop and walk a bit, but when you next try it run a little further. Do that each time until you make it. If your breathing gets panicky, take a deep breath and then blow air out through your mouth. The advantage of running up a hill, apart from making you stronger, is that once you get to the top, it's then downward all the way, and as you run downhill you will recover. As you get fitter, you can decide whether to attack hills at a hard run, or to maintain a steady pace.

And, finally, run at your own pace. As a general rule, for most beginners a comfortable, realistic speed is about 8 to 12 minutes a mile. You have plenty of time to build up to a faster speed if you want to.

Where to run

The marvellous thing about running is that you can do it anywhere – on a track, along the street, in parks, the countryside or by the seashore. I'm lucky enough to live in a town which contains all of these – which is probably one of the main reasons why I don't want to move away – but not all runners have that amount of choice. I started running in the park opposite my house, around a hilly 1-mile route. Claudia, by contrast, began running around a track, one lap equalling a quarter-mile. It had the advantage of being a measured distance, but track running can become boring. Once Claudia had gained sufficient confidence and could run four laps, or one mile, she switched to running on the roads.

Where you run obviously depends on where you live and what facilities are available. If you live in the country, there are roads, paths, tracks, fields and woods. Even the most urban centre usually contains a park somewhere but if it doesn't you can run around the block or find an interesting street route – running is the best possible way to explore an area. If you are not using a track but do want to know how far you are running, or want to set yourself a specific goal, then you can measure out a distance first in a car or on a bicycle by using a milometer, or by working out a measured run with the help of an ordnance survey map.

All kinds of weather

For some people the weather dictates their running, although it never determines mine. I'll run in the rain, snow, wind or heat; each one is an experience and a very natural thing to do. In many ways I particularly enjoy running in so-called bad weather; women are forced to spend so much time worrying about their appearance, the rain spoiling a new hair style, or the wind blowing hair off our faces, exposing perhaps features we are not very fond of, such as the odd spot, big ears or a large nose. For women, running in all weathers is a very liberating experience, so don't be put off by rain or cold.

Running should be fun and certainly to run with other people in bad weather can be both fun and exhilarating. On one occasion a group of us went for a hard run through driving rain. Quite without noticing it, we began to mark the run by puddles, seeing who would get to the next puddle first and jump into it, splashing the others.

Snow and ice do present some problems and you may have to slow your pace to prevent slipping. Even so they can also be enjoyable. All you need are a few extra layers of clothing, and once again you can liven things up by jumping up to touch tree branches, bringing down small avalanches of snow onto yourself or other runners.

All weather conditions add something to your abilities as a runner. Running against the wind, for instance, can be hard but is good resistance training, while running with the wind behind you is a wonderful feeling, making you run very quickly. Fog may present some problems, some asthma sufferers may experience breathing difficulties because of the damp. Eileen, a running friend who suffers from asthma, prefers not to let it interfere with her running, and just makes sure to take her Intal inhaler before her run. Also, if fog is really dense, choose a route you know well.

Hot weather causes more difficulties than cold. It can be tiring and you will certainly sweat more. Perhaps wear a head band and put vaseline on your eyebrows to stop sweat falling into your eyes. Carry a handkerchief or piece of rag to wipe your brow, and wear a sun-hat to protect your head. If you burn easily, then put sun-cream on your legs, arms and any other exposed parts of your body. If you are going on a long run, drink some water, fruit or vegetable juice before you go, or carry a small plastic bottle full of water or juice in a zip pouch attached to a running belt. Sweating is the body's way of regulating heat but problems can occur if you dehydrate, that is if your body loses more fluid than it takes in (see page 111). If you are someone who really dislikes the heat, then run in the early morning or during the evening.

What to wear

When I started running there weren't as many cheap track suits around as there are today, and they certainly weren't fashionable; in fact I had never heard the term 'jogging' in those days. I began running in loose-fitting jeans and an old T-shirt; for a start I didn't feel like a runner so I didn't want to look like one. Also, being in ordinary clothes, I could stop and walk whenever I wanted to, and nobody need know I had been running. Eventually I bought myself a pair of stretch trousers and then, finally, when I had enough confidence, I dared to put on shorts. I certainly wasn't as brave as Mary who put on shorts the first day she ran.

A runner's wardrobe consists of trainers, T-shirt, shorts and track suit, but there is no need to rush out and buy all the expensive clothing on offer; most of the running gear can be bought in a street market or well-known chain store. Sweat tops and track suit bottoms can be found on every market stall and fairly cheaply. Jogging bottoms can be bought at stalls quite cheaply. And you might even have suitable clothes tucked away in your wardrobe, something old and stretchy.

To start with you don't really want to be too conspicuous. Whatever you wear should be comfortable, loose-fitting and light.

Shoes

Feet are important; they carry the body around and cannot be replaced. When you run a mile, each foot in turn has to support the entire weight of your body more than 1,000 times. If you run just 2 miles a day, by the end of a year, each foot will have hit the ground 650,000 times. Shoes are therefore crucial. Lots of runners, including myself and Claudia, started their running in plimsolls, but it is wise to buy a pair of training shoes (trainers) to protect your feet. Most of us haven't got grass to train on, and wearing plimsolls on hard ground will not absorb the shock when your foot hits the ground as trainers will. Although barefoot running has become the fashion, it is not advisable, except, perhaps, on grass.

Choose your shoes carefully and if possible try them on in the late afternoon when your feet are at their largest. Also, when you try them on, wear the sort of socks that you may be running in. When you run, your foot spreads as it takes the weight of your body, so always choose shoes that allow for this spread.

POINTS TO LOOK FOR

SHAPE AND FIT: The shoe you choose should follow the contour of your foot. Make sure that it is wide enough for your forefoot as your foot will spread as you run. The shoe should be deep enough for your big toe, and the inside should be smooth so that your toe-nail does not snag, yet resilient and soft so that your toe is cushioned. The shoe should also be deep enough to allow sufficient space for the central arch or highest point of your foot. The tongue should be high enough not to slip backwards, and should be padded to prevent friction.

The heel should be reinforced and should provide firm support for your heel bone. Most trainers have a protruding heel tab – often as a means of advertising the maker's name. This should come no higher up than the ankle joint, any higher and it will damage the achilles tendon. If you cannot find shoes without a heel tab, it is a good idea to make vertical cuts either side of the tab down to the level of your ankle. This will prevent friction.

Soles and uppers should be the same width in all parts of the shoe. Look at the shoe from underneath; if the upper overlaps the sole, then the sole will not support your foot. The sole should be of constant thickness and flexible, but firm under the heel. The insole should be soft and firm. If you are flat-footed, you can get shoes with a built-in padding to support the inner arch. Choose shoes that are well-ventilated, that can 'breathe'. Avoid excessive plastic trimmings as these cause the feet to overheat. lightweight trainers will be adequate for short distance, or speed running; for long distances you will need something heavier and more durable. You will need spiked shoes if you eventually intend to do track or cross-country running. Make sure that they have a slight heel.

WHICH MAKE?   While running certainly leads to fitness, bad shoes can cause serious foot, leg or back problems. There is an enormous and bewildering range of trainers to choose from today, and the most expensive are not necessarily the best. I tend to run on the sole of my foot, rather than rolling from heel to toe which is the best style. And the shoe which has given me a more balanced style is the Nike Yankee, usually priced about £22. Hi-Tec shoes are reasonably cheap and fairly good value but tend to be rather wide fitting. Well-known makes such as Adidas, Brooks, Dunlop, Nike and Reebok all produce reasonable women's trainers with narrower fittings. What is surprising, and patronising, however, is that so many women's trainers are produced in pastel pinks and blues as if women never run in the rain or through mud and dirt!

So confusing is the range of sports shoes that in June 1984 the British *Which?* magazine did their own survey, and it is a very useful guide. They tested a variety of running and training shoes ranging in price from £7-£40. Their main aim was to look at shoes intended for general running, jogging or training rather than for the more committed runner, and they were looking in particular for those shoes providing the greatest comfort, support and durability. According to their findings, there is no such thing as the 'perfect' running shoe, instead you get what you pay for according to your needs. Of those that they examined, the best of the most expensive (over £25) were the Adidas Oregon, Brooks Super Villanova and Brooks Vantage. For women who run or jog regularly, they recommend the women's Nike Spirit, Adidas Lady Boston, Reebok Orchid, or unisex Hi-Tec Silver Shadow, Adidas Seattle, and the Nike Yankee (prices from £18 to about £23). And among the cheaper ranges (under £15), for those who do low-mileage jogging, they recommend the Power Nevada, Dunlop Lady Superstar and the Hi-Tec Runaway. As a final tip, never send away for a pair of training shoes unless you know they fit and you have worn that make before.

Clothes

The clothes you wear will depend to some extent on the weather, although remember that if you start off cold, you are likely to be warm within about 15 minutes. If you feel cold at the start of a run, wear a sweat shirt or something you can take off later and tie around your waist. Running magazines often advertise sports clothing, but never send away for any item unless you know exactly what you are buying and are certain of size and quality.

T-SHIRTS   These can be of cotton, nylon or a mixed cotton and artificial fibres. Cotton is more absorbent than nylon, although I find a nylon singlet is best for a long run in hot weather as it doesn't get wet and soggy with sweat. I also prefer loose-fitting T-shirts. Wear what you find is most comfortable, and again there is no need to lash out on expensive logo-emblazoned running tops; you have probably got something quite suitable in your wardrobe.

SHORTS   Only a few years ago women's running briefs caused an outcry among the then running fraternity; today, at last, they are quite acceptable, and they are ideal for running. Avoid shorts that are tight fitting with zips and belts, instead choose a comfortable pair of cotton or nylon shorts with an elasticated waist. Shorts with slits at the sides are available and give extra freedom. There is a wide range available in sports shops, but you will probably find cheaper alternatives elsewhere. If you join a local athletic, jogging or running club you will normally qualify for a discount at your local sports shop.

BRAS   Wearing a bra is a matter of personal choice. Some women find it too uncomfortable to run without a bra, others never wear one for running. Personally I do wear a bra and have no particular preference. Sports bras are available today. They are elasticated bras with few seams and no fastenings so that rubbing or chafing is reduced. However, in this area as in so many others, women runners are not being taken seriously. Warners, one of Britain's leading lingerie manufacturers, produce their own sports bra, a one-piece without any metal fittings that, according to their horrendous advertising both 'takes the jiggle out of jogging', and avoids the 'boobs' that have been made by earlier bras. Many women are already sufficiently embarrassed about their breasts without this sort of insulting patronage. As Cathy Gibb, journalist and sportswoman, has pointed out, slogans such as these are not only incorrect, they also exploit, undermine and insult women. Warners have clearly neglected to produce any protective clothing for men, and it would be interesting to know whether a man's jock strap would be described in such a snappy way!

If you do decide to get a sports bra – and they are also manufactured by Berlie and Triumph – make sure you try it on first. If you have any difficulties with size, and find that elasticated bras do not provide sufficient support, go to a specialist lingerie shop, explain what you are looking for and what price you want to pay.

SOCKS   Socks protect your feet from rubbing against your shoe and raising blisters, and are an extra means of protection against impact. Socks also absorb sweat. Cotton socks are most suitable but nylon or mixed fibre varieties are also available. Running socks are best if you are going to increase your mileage; I find that ordinary socks tend to fall down, rub and bunch under my heel which is most uncomfortable. As with shoes, make sure your socks are the right fit.

OTHER USEFUL TIMES   In wet weather an ordinary track suit can become waterlogged, heavy and uncomfortable. Rainproof anoraks can be bought fairly cheaply and are useful for wind, rain and snow. Rainproof suits, however, can trap sweat inside them, so, if you can afford it, it may be a good investment to pay out for one of the new all-weather waterproof suits such as the 'Gortex' suits which are specially designed to allow sweat to evaporate while keeping rain out and the body perfectly dry. If it is not too cold, a rain top and shorts are quite adequate – always remember that the skin is, itself, waterproof.

In cold weather a wooly hat, gloves, a warm top and track suit bottoms will keep you beautifully warm. A warm scarf may also be useful.

Check that your shoes have good grips to avoid slipping in either snow or mud.

Other useful items include nylon pouches with zip fasteners that can be attached to a belt and which can be used to carry money, a small towel, a spare T-shirt or perhaps a drink.

A small, lighweight rucksack may also be useful if you want to carry a change of clothes, or a towel.

What not to wear

Do not wear:
1   tight, restricted clothing; running is for freedom and movement so take the opportunity to be as free and unrestricted as possible;
2   large earrings with hanging drops; they knock against the

side of the jaw which is uncomfortable and distracting; alternatively they may fall off;

3 make-up and moisturiser; they clog the skin, and when you sweat or if it rains, eye make-up in particular will streak and may sting the eyes;

4 hair gel; again this will sting the eyes when you sweat and can be uncomfortable and painful.

Organising your day

You should run before you eat, or at least 2 hours afterwards; running on a full stomach is uncomfortable and the body needs the energy to digest. Drinking before you run is alright, although you will feel any liquid sloshing about inside you for a while.

What time of day you choose for your run is very much your own preference. A lot depends on whether you have children or not, whether you are single or have a partner, or whether you work outside the home. Some women prefer to run in the very early morning, say at about 6 or 7am, and this can perhaps be the best time if you live in a very busy or heavily polluted area. It is a quiet time of the day and, if you have children and a partner who will look after them, gives you a chance to run before they get up. Your body will need time to adjust, however, so you should get up about three-quarters of an hour before your run.

Childcare can be a major problem for women who want to run. Women who have pre-school children at play group or toddler group can organise a run while the children are occupied. If other mothers in the group also want to run, you could try organising a rota so that some women run while others look after the children. The same principle can apply to women with very young children at home; sharing childcare is often the solution to the problem of finding time to run. If you can team up with a friend or friends, one or two of you can look after the children while the others run, and then you can swop around. Organising this can take time but it is worth it, and there's no need to feel guilty about leaving children for a while. If you run regularly, children soon get accustomed to the idea and learn to know that it is your time to run and to be on your own. Alternatively, you may find that your children want to run with you. In fact, it was partly through my running that I came to realise how little is done to help parents to have any time for themselves; caring for children 24 hours a day can be a soul-destroying job leaving parents with very little personal freedom. We are, however, made to feel very guilty if we ever admit to this; how much better it would be if governments spent more time and money on nurseries, creches and other childcare facilities than on weapons that destroy.

Many waged women find that the lunch hour is a good time to run, it certainly makes the afternoon shorter. A nearby park or green space is ideal; failing that a run around the block or from the local sports centre might be possible. During my lunchtime I used to run through a field near my school; now, however, I have less time so I run to the school in the morning and back again after work, an overall distance of about 4 miles. I run in my gear, carrying my working clothes in a small rucksack on my back, and wash and change when I get to work. Alternatively you could keep spare clothes at work.

Beginner's schedule

Like most other runners, when I first started I pushed myself too hard but at the time I only had men to run with as I knew no other

... your children may want to run with you ...

women runners. Men are not as patient, and are reluctant to maintain a slower pace so, like others, I gasped for breath at the end of each run. But I felt so good afterwards that I went out and repeated the exercise time and time again, determined to get on top of this running. It was painful to begin with and there was some discomfort but to quote Claudia's advice to new runners: 'Don't worry, it's only pain'. And it does go away.

Now you've organised your day, and you have found your time to run, you can begin to follow the schedule below. Keep jogging at a steady pace. The schedule is only a guide line; instead of rigid clock-watching, add those extra minutes by using lamp posts, gates or trees as incentives to run a little further. Either jog out from the house and walk back, or jog out for just a few minutes, and then jog back. Your beginner's schedule could jog along like this:

DAY	WEEK 1	WEEK 2	WEEK 3	WEEK 4	WEEK 5
1	5 mins	5 mins	8 mins	8 mins	10 mins
2	5 mins	8 mins	10 mins	5 mins	5 mins
3	7 mins	5 mins	5 mins	12 mins	15 mins
4	5 mins	8 mins	10 mins	10 mins	8 mins
5	7 mins	5 mins	5 mins	5 mins	5 mins
6	rest	rest	rest	rest	rest
7	8 mins	10 mins	12 mins	12 to 15 mins	15 mins

DAY	WEEK 6	WEEK 7	WEEK 8	WEEK 9	WEEK 10
1	10 mins	12 mins	12 mins	10 mins	12 mins
2	8 mins	8 mins	8 mins	15 mins	18 mins
3	15 mins	18 mins	18 mins	10 mins	10 mins
4	8 mins	8 mins	12 mins	18 mins	18 mins
5	10 mins	10 mins	10 mins	10 mins	10 mins
6	rest	rest	rest	rest	rest
7	18 mins	18 mins	20 mins	20 mins	20 mins

You don't have to keep rigidly to this schedule. Take rest days when you need them, for instance if your body is too stiff to jog – your body does need recovery days. Build up slowly. Once you come to the end of the schedule, you can run for 20 minutes, then gradually build up a little more, first to 25 and then 30 minutes.

Once you start your schedule keep a diary. It should be prepared ready for your return because it is important to note improvement or feelings you have during or after your run. It should be kept something like this:

DATE	TRAINING	COMMENT
11.11.84	20 mins jog	Felt great the best I have felt didn't stop to walk
12.11.84	10 mins jog	A bit stiff thought it better to do a short jog.

Minor problems

You may notice some minor problems when you start to run:

BREATHLESSNESS: don't run until you are completely out of breath; it will only make you panic. Instead, if you get breathless, stop, walk and breathe slowly and deeply. This will relax you and once you are breathing normally, you can start running again.

STITCH: this can be very painful. It doesn't only happen to novice runners and is often caused by incorrect breathing. You can either stop and massage the affected area, or just carry on jogging at a very slow pace. Either way the pain will disappear on its own.

LEAKAGE OF URINE: Some women, particularly those who have had children, find that they dribble some urine when they run. The same thing can happen when they cough or laugh. It is usually the result of a weakness in the pelvic muscles brought on by childbearing, and there is not much that can be done to cure it. Exercises may help; otherwise women who are affected should check that they have emptied their bladder before running, and may need to wear a pad.

FARTING: breaking wind or needing to go to the lavatory are perfectly normal occurrences when you run; in fact public toilets are a runner's best friend; going to the lavatory makes a break during your run, and can provide amusement if there is some good graffiti on the walls.

SWEATING: sweating when you run is also absolutely normal, in fact it is a sure sign that you are exercising your body. Although we are conditioned to believe sweating is 'unladylike', it is the body's natural means of heat regulation and also helps to rid the body of waste products. If you sweat excessively you will need to drink a lot of water before and after you run. There are special electrolyte drinks for runners that contain essential nutrients lost through sweat. When I'm hot, sweaty and thirsty my favourite drink is a fruit juice and soda water, water can be a bit bland.

ACHING MUSCLES: if you are new to running and to exercise generally, you can expect to get some aches and pains as your unfit body adjusts. Hot baths, massage and gentle exercise will

"If you'd just stand still, my dog won't chase you..."

help and most aches should disappear quite quickly. if pain persists, or becomes too severe, you may be overdoing your running.

IRRITATION: sweating may sometimes cause clothes to chafe or rub, for instance on the inside of your thighs. Some runners apply vaseline as a means of prevention, particularly on vulnerable areas such as the inner tops of thighs, nipples or under the breasts.

Helpful ideas

TRY AND RUN AT THE SAME TIME EVERY DAY so that you and your body get into a regular routine. Be disciplined and fairly strict with yourself. There will be days when you don't feel like running, when you feel tired, harassed, or just can't be bothered. It may be that you have done too much running and need a rest. But if not, make the effort to run, it will be worth it and you will feel a new you when you get back.

DOGS: dogs are enemy number 1 for all runners whether women or men. I wonder just how many runners have had dogs chase them, bark or growl at them while their owners just stand by with such comments as 'It won't hurt you', or 'If you would just stand still, then my dog won't chase you', or, even worse 'He's only playing', as the dog takes a great nip out of your leg! If you are harassed by dogs, try to get the owner's address; by law dogs should be under control and if they are not, their owners should be reported. I myself have done this several times, and have written to my local council who in turn have sent warning letters to the relevant dog owners. Try not to be frightened when you run past a dog, it will sense your fear and chase you, so stay calm but alert as dogs often attack from behind. Other running friends of mine have shouted, kicked or struck out at dogs although this usually upsets their owners. Unfortunately there is no one solution to this problem which will obviously remain until some owners become more responsible.

SEXUAL HARASSMENT: Many women runners suffer attacks not only from dogs but also from men. Sexual harassment of one sort or another, usually verbal but sometimes physical, is a major problem for all women, runners or not, and unfortunately, won't disappear until sexist social attitudes do. One woman runner has suggested that there should be a curfew on men so that they are not allowed out after 6pm – a good idea but unfortunately harassment can happen at any time of the day or night. There are various ways of dealing with the problem, either to challenge it or to run away from it but it is probably best to avoid confrontation.

It is probably also best to run with others rather than on your own, and to carry some form of defence item such as an aerosol, lemon spray, pepper and so on which can be used if a direct attack is made, and meanwhile kept close at hand in your runner's pouch belt. However, the more you run, the stronger, faster and more confident you become as a woman. I am far less concerned about harassment now, for no other reason than that I know I can run fast – a major advantage in a man's world!

RUNNING AT NIGHT: if you run at night, again it is probably advisable to run with someone else. Also you must wear a reflective vest or light-coloured clothing which can be clearly seen by car drivers. If you are running on the roads at night, always face on-coming traffic.

Diet

I lost weight when I started running and so have many other women. But not all of us do. Val, for instance, says

> 'a lot of other runners look so slimlined, but I weigh just as much if not more than ever, being a compulsive eater. It hasn't cured me of that. I have the energy to do more things but I wonder if I could run faster if there was less of me. I am fit but I don't always look it'.

As women, most of us are obsessed and anxious about our weight and body shape which is a shame. There is no one perfect shape or size – we are all different and wouldn't it be a shame if we weren't? For many women the main attraction of exercise is that it is supposed to burn off excess weight. But this can only happen if your energy input is less than your energy needs. If you eat more than you burn in energy you will stay the same weight.

What is much more important is that we should liberate our bodies whatever their shape, to be free and healthy. Running is the means to this end but what you eat also remains important. That is true whether you are a runner or not, but there is no point in running and ignoring the quality of what you eat.

The more you run, however, the more body-aware you will become and the more you will want to treat your body kindly. This means you will probably want to consider what the best foods are. There are plenty of books and pamphlets around today on diet and nutrition so there is no point in repeating detailed information here. The last few years, however, have seen an alarming rise of heart disorders among women, and there is little doubt that cholesterol plays a major part in this increase. In the United States, in January 1984, a twelve-year study into the connection between cholesterol and heart disease was completed and its findings were reported in the magazine *Runner's World*. According to the study, 'there can no longer be any doubt that cholesterol causes heart disease'. As a result it is advisable to avoid saturated or animal fats such as butter, cream or lard in favour of polyunsaturated fats such as vegetable oils – soya, corn, sunflower or safflower. Other foods recommended for a healthy diet include high-fibre cereals, fresh fruit, vegetables, wholemeal foods, nuts, grains, beans, lentils and so on. All of them contain minerals and vitamins required for health, and all of them are relatively fat free. For the same reason, dairy foods should be eaten only moderately, and increasingly there is emphasis on low-fat varieties such as skimmed milk, natural yoghurt and low-fat cheese such as cottage cheese or Edam.

I personally am a vegetarian but many runners eat meat quite happily. There is no hard and fast rule. Opinions are divided as to whether runners need extra protein, minerals or vitamins. Some experts say yes, others say no. I personally take a few vitamin supplements – Vitamin C and Vitamin B6 and also take extra iron, but these are a matter of personal choice. Only in one case is there a specialised diet. Known as 'The Diet' it is used by some marathon runners who, about a week before a marathon, run 20 miles or more to use up the body's store of glycogen (food in the form used directly by muscles). Then they eat a low-carbohydrate diet for three or four days, followed by a high-carbohydrate diet for the period up to the race. Known as 'carbohydrate loading', this builds up the body's store of glycogen to a higher level than normal and prevents a marathon runner from 'hitting the wall', a term used to describe a collapse that can occur about 20 to 23 miles into the race when the glycogen store is depleted.

9 *KEEP ON RUNNING*

By now you are well on the way to jogging a regular 20 to 30 minutes three times a week. This will keep you fit, and will give you time to yourself to enjoy either on your own or with a friend. If you have been running regularly do you feel different? Are you looking forward to your runs? Did you time your first continuous run? Does it take less time now? Does it feel easier? The chances are that you've answered 'yes' to these questions, and that you are probably feeling a lot better than you were a month or six weeks ago. Let's see what is happening to your body:

The human machine: running and your body

Your body is like a well-made machine, and like a machine it needs good and constant maintenance so that it functions efficiently and so that you will be able to get the most out of it. Through running that is exactly what you are doing because running affects some of the most important organs of the body, the heart, blood vessels and lungs. Or, more technically, the cardiovascular and respiratory systems.

Running is an *aerobic* exercise, a descriptive term coined by Dr Kenneth Cooper, an American fitness expert. The word 'aerobic' itself literally means 'with air', and describes any *sustained* exercise such as running which improves the ability of the heart and lungs to supply oxygen to the body's tissues, and particularly the muscles. The body needs oxygen all the time because any activity uses up energy, and energy itself is released by the continual metabolism of food fuels: the 'burning' up of glucose and fatty acids by oxygen. Therefore, the better the supply of oxygen to the body and the more efficiently it can be delivered to the body's tissues, the more energy can be produced.

And that's exactly what running does. The key to its success is that running or jogging, as opposed to say sprinting, is a sustained exercise. If you run at a steady and sustained pace for one or more miles, your muscles work harder, your oxygen needs increase, you breathe hard and deep for a sustained period, and your heart beats faster. In effect you are making your body work harder, and by doing so are improving its efficiency. Take the heart, for instance. It

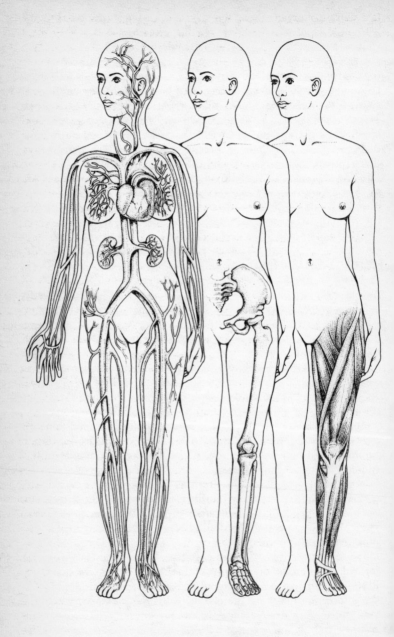

Figure 9.1 *The human machine*

is a muscular organ, about the size of your fist, that pumps blood continuously around the body, via the circulatory system. The heart itself is divided into its left and right sides by a muscular wall. Each side contains two chambers, the upper called the atrium, the lower the ventricle. The blood flow between these four chambers is controlled by four heart valves. The blood carries oxygen and nutrients to the various parts of the body and also removes waste products. In the space of a single heart beat, freshly oxygenated blood arriving from the lungs enters the left side of the heart to be dispersed to all the body's organs and tissues, while 'stale' or deoxygenated blood is pumped out of the right side of the heart to the lungs where carbon dioxide and other waste products are exchanged for oxygen.

About 5 litres (9 pints) of blood flow continuously around the body, but how it is distributed depends on what we are doing. When the body is resting, or fairly inactive, most of the blood flow goes to internal organs dealing with digestion and so on. During exercise, however, as when you are running, blood flow is largely diverted to those muscles which are doing extra work and so require more oxygen. As the demand for oxygen increases, the heart beats faster, pumping more blood, and your pulse rate increases. As you do more running, and get fitter, your heart becomes more efficient at pumping blood. Even though your pulse rate will still increase when you are running, it will be slower than before. When you are fit the amount of blood pushed through your heart with each beat can be half as much again as before you started running. As a result fewer total strokes of the heart are required to meet the oxygen needs of your resting body.

An unfit person's heart beats, on average, between 80 and 100 times a minute when they are resting; by contrast a marathon runner's heart may beat as few as 40 to 50 times a minute. Through running your heart is becoming larger, stronger and more efficient, less prone to fatigue and to strain. At the same time your entire cardiovascular system is also improving as the number and size of the blood vessels in your body are actually increasing, so helping to prevent dangers such as hardening of the arteries and high blood pressure. Through running the cardiovascular system improves its blood-carrying ability, as more capillaries (small blood vessels) are formed to improve the supply of food and oxygen to the body. Running burns up excess fats too. This checks the deposit of fats in the arteries so reducing the risk of thrombosis. Through running your respiratory system becomes more efficient and, your lungs increase in size and capacity. Finally, running also improves the strength and endurance capabilities of your muscles, particularly the abdominal, arm and leg muscles. The overall effect is not only to improve your body but also to make you feel better.

Checking your pulse

You can actually monitor your improved fitness by checking your pulse rate to measure the number of times your heart beats in a minute. The more efficient your circulatory and respiratory systems are, the less furiously they have to work during exercise, and the quicker they return to normal afterwards.

To check your resting pulse rate, choose a time when you are relaxed and calm and sitting or lying down. Place the first three fingers of one hand on the inside of the other wrist, level with the base of the thumb. You should be able to feel your pulse. Count the number of beats in either 15 or 30 seconds and multiply by 4 or 2 respectively to find the number of beats in a minute. Over the weeks and months of running your resting pulse rate will go down as your cardiovascular system gets more efficient.

What next? Keeping going

So, that is what is happening to your body. If you've managed to get through your beginner's schedule, and have continued to run despite some initial discomfort such as breathlessness, stitch, and maybe even a little pain, and if you are still feeling good about running, that's great. You are now a runner.

The next step is to keep going. If you go out running because you think you 'should' do it, that it will be 'good' for you, or even just to lose weight, running will become a chore and it is unlikely you will stick at it. It takes a long time to get fit; it doesn't happen in a matter of weeks but takes months. It also takes some women longer than others to adjust to running, and it often happens when you least expect it. I remember when a friend of mine started running. Two months later she was still finding our regular 2¼-mile run a struggle and was about to give up because she felt she wasn't getting anywhere. But the very day she decided to do her last run, that 2¼ miles suddenly became easy and she carried on running after all. So, keep trying, you will make it; already you've achieved something you've never done before.

Don't forget that like any other sport, running is a discipline; time has to be set aside for it and it needs to be a regular event. If you start to miss out runs, it can be hard getting back into the routine.

And even if you've been running for some months, restarting after a break can be almost as hard as starting from scratch. If you've not done so already, now is the time to make a regular arrangement to run with a friend or friends. Or join a club that caters for joggers. It's worth remembering what Claudia said, that running isn't something that you 'should' do, it's something to be enjoyed. Running is special, it is not a chore that has to be done, so make it part of your life.

Making choices

If you are running three times a week for 20 minutes each time, at a 10-minute mile pace, that means you are probably running about 6 miles (10km) a week, which is excellent. Six miles a week, once you are fit, will certainly keep you so, and may well be the weekly routine you want. Many women, however, find that this is not enough, that they want to improve in some way or another – to get faster, run further, or to vary their running patterns. There are a number of directions that you can go in – you can carry on as you are, increase your distance, aim for a fun run, road race or marathon, take up orienteering. Once you start running, all sorts of possibilities open up. Most of them are discussed in the following pages – which one you choose is up to you.

Putting up your distance – getting a 'bigger dose'

While it is true that actual distance isn't that important, most of us like to be able to tell others how far we've run, and to set goals to run a little further. Certainly, I remember the feelings of pleasure and achievement when I told my friends that I had run 2, then 3 and then 4 miles – it was a completely new and exciting feeling.

Again, to increase your distance, you should build up gradually. When you start to run further, do it using the same principle as before when you were building up your time; do a longer run one day, followed by a shorter run the next. Be careful not to overdo it. Run every other day if the longer runs make you tired. As you have decided to run further, always run in an easy and relaxed way and, if necessary, walk for a bit. Take notice of your body and ease off if it seems to be too difficult. If you want to find out how far you've run, an Ordnance Survey map is very useful. At home we use a piece of string and wind it round the roads on the map to measure our runs. Alternative methods are to check the distance with a car or bicycle and a mileometer.

Running is a very rhythmic exercise; there is nothing better than going out for a really long run and, after about half an hour, finding that whatever you have been worrying about no longer bothers you. You are warmed up, running easily and into a good, steady pace. It is now that you can get used to a 'bigger dose' to quote Kathleen, a fifty-two year old running friend. I often get a real urge to run 10 miles or more; it actually does blow the cobwebs away.

Thinking about racing – you don't have to be good

A race or fun run might seem a daunting prospect, but today women and men of all ages and very differing abilities are running in them – you don't have to be good. When I started there weren't that many women running. The only all-women races were the cross-country or short 2 to 5-mile road races. Now there is a wide choice of fun runs and women-only road races, their distances ranging from 1 mile to 50 miles or more.

Races and fun runs are very good ways to improve your speed and times. They provide a goal and the excitement of the big occasion is very stimulating. Running requires self-discipline but sometimes we all need a little extra incentive to get out of the door and run – commitment to a running group maybe, or the target of a fun run may be just what we need to keep us going.

My younger sister, I'm proud to say, recently started racing. She saw an advertisement for the British Nike/*Woman's Own* 6-mile (10km) fun run and decided to have a go. She did just enough training to cover the distance and on the day enjoyed the run so much that she now describes herself as 'addicted'. She's right – racing is addictive; it is extremely enjoyable and gets you out again, training for the next race.

One of the best things about events such as these is that they are social occasions, gatherings of people who are all there for one purpose – to run – and all interested in each other's achievements. The same faces turn up again and again. We get to know each other, can talk about training, the latest races and how we are feeling.

All sorts of people are running today, and you may even have the chance to run with international runners as Chris did during her first 10-mile road race. The race was over a three-lap course.

Inevitably in a race over several laps, the fastest runners do lap the slowest which is what happened to Chris. She was steadily jogging around her second lap when a man whizzed past her on his third and final lap. Chris turned to the person running beside her saying 'He's bloody good', to which the other runner replied, 'Well, it is Steve Ovett!'. Chris remembers that he was waiting at the finish cheering the other runners in.

I've also had memorable experiences during road races. In November 1983 I ran in a 10-mile road race, and was enormously inspired to find myself running with a blind runner and his partner. Today there are quite a number of blind runners; they run with a sighted partner, both holding on to the end of a short cord. More recently I did a 2-mile run in Hastings. I didn't particularly feel like racing that day. An up and coming international athlete, Bridget Smythe, was also racing. I decided to go off slowly but got into the race and started catching runners up including the leaders, one of whom was Bridget. I overtook them and Bridget, who could easily have forged right ahead to achieve a course record, came with me. We continued running together, talking, laughing and joking: it turned out to be a very enjoyable fast run. At the finish Bridget moved into first position, and I came second.

On long races too there is always someone to run with, woman or man, and it helps you to keep going. In 1983 I ran a 20-mile road race in Worthing, England, and found myself running with a man who had finished just behind me in a half-marathon the week before. We talked for a while as we were running, and then decided on a pace that suited both of us so that we could carry on together, in effect 'pulling' each other around the distance.

Women in races often find themselves surrounded by men running at the same pace because, although some of them might prefer a much slower and easier pace, many men are reluctant to be beaten by a woman and desperately try to keep up. For a woman runner, of course, it is very encouraging to beat men: one woman, describing the pleasures she gets from running, says: 'At last I can beat the man in my life', and a lot of other women would know just what she means. More often than not, however, I have been congratulated by a man if I have had a tussle with him during a race and have beaten him.

Fear of competition puts a lot of women off racing but in my experience running is not highly competitive. Instead, as Claudia described, there is a feeling of comradeship in running. Also women are often worried about what they are going to look like, but nobody in a fun run is judging or comparing anyone else: instead your thoughts turn to whether you can keep the pace up, certain that you can't. Amazingly enough you will find you can keep the pace up, you can get through and feel okay. At the finish everybody is pleased, happy and smiling, we just feel proud of ourselves and our achievements.

Being prepared: the need for training

In 1960 Wilma Rudolph, the American sprinter and gold medallist was asked: 'How come you run so fast?'. 'Man', she flashed with a smile, 'in my family you hadda run fast if you wanted to eat!'.

For most of us running to survive is not an issue, although given the sexual and other harassment that women face, I think the ability to run fast should be every woman's aim. That apart, however, once you have done a few fun runs or races, or even before, you will probably want to improve your running and to get faster, especially if you want to take racing a little more seriously. Over the next few pages we've described various training methods. Pick out a few ideas, try them and then stick to them. Build up your training slowly, your body needs time to adjust to the new work load, and to the new speed. Remember too that what suits one woman might not suit another.

Jimmy Green, a British coach, recalls when junior women (under fifteen) were first permitted to race over cross-country courses:

> 'At the finish bodies were lying everywhere – I described it in *Athletics Weekly* [a British athletics magazine] as like a battlefield; it was due to many women being allowed by not-very-knowledgeable officials or coaches to run when not properly trained. We soon taught them not to run unless they had done the training and not to flop down at the end of the race . . .'

The main purpose of training then is to help you get stronger, faster and to help you overcome weaknesses in your running. It is also to make sure that you can cover the distance of whichever event you enter properly prepared and without distress. The amount of time you put into training depends on the amount of time you have, and the amount of running you have already done. Speed work is hard and it requires that you should already have strengthened your cardiovascular system. Long, steady runs of between 6 to 20 miles once or twice a week is the best way of doing this. When I started, I didn't do any specific speed training; instead I did seven months of long, steady runs (about 6 miles on average) or cross-country races, sometimes pushing myself particularly hard when I joined the men of our local athletic's club for part of their runs. I couldn't keep up with them for the whole distance then, nor did we have a woman's running club at that time. After the seven months, I joined in some speedwork sessions on the track with the men, doing what is known as repetition running over 200 or 300 metres. It was very hard, particularly training with men.

At that time, seven years ago, I had very little idea about training or what was happening to my body. I didn't realise then that those long, steady runs were an aerobic exercise and that they were helping my body to work more efficiently. I only knew that I felt good and that I was getting stronger. This build-up of mileage also made my speedwork easier because my body was able to recover more quickly.

After a while I began to read up on various types of training. There are many different schools of thought about training – some coaches or runners believe in quality work, that is fast, short runs; others believe in quantity work – longer, steady running. In the end the person who impressed me most was Arthur Lydiard, the New Zealand runner, coach and writer. He advocates a good, basic groundwork of steady running which he calls conditioning training and which is something that I agree with. His work has influenced many runners and coaches, and what is more, he has tried out his methods on himself.

Below are some commonly-used methods of training that will probably equip you for any race you may try. If you want to expand your training you will find plenty of books on the subject. Or you may even want to try and get your own coach; sadly, there are very few top female coaches and we very rarely hear anything about them.

Training

There are four basic elements to a runner's training programme – stamina (or endurance), speed, suppleness and strength.

STAMINA TRAINING is the long, steady aerobic running that is essential for the longer-distance events. After an initial warming-up period, you run for half an hour or more at a steady pace, but not so fast that you feel breathless. Steady running is aerobic exercise in that there is a balance between the oxygen taken in by the lungs and the oxygen needed for fuel by the muscles. You can run, therefore, at a constant pace without having to stop to get your breath back.

SPEED TRAINING involves running fast, or sprinting, then resting to recover, then running fast again. This form of training can be *anaerobic* (literally 'without air') inasmuch as you may run fast enough to get out of breath, then have to stop to get your breath back again. What happens is that when you start off running fast, your muscles are being supplied with oxygen that is already being carried around your body in your blood. As you continue sprinting this oxygen is used up, your muscles 'run out of fuel', your oxygen needs become greater than your oxygen intake, and you have to slow down and breathe deeply, or pant, to get as much oxygen from your lungs into your bloodstream as you can, so that your muscles have more fuel to work with. The term 'oxygen debt' is often used to describe this state. After a few minutes rest, the amount of oxygen in your blood will be back to normal, you will be breathing normally, and you can go and do another burst of sprinting.

SUPPLENESS TRAINING exercises the joints over their full range of movement and is useful to help relaxation before going off on a run. Running itself is a repetitive action, and involves the joints in only a limited range of movements. In order that your body does not become too restricted in movement, it is advisable to do a range of mobilising and stretching exercises (see page 106) such as arm circling and toe touching.

STRENGTH TRAINING makes specific groups of muscles stronger. Some runners do weight training to strengthen their legs and arm muscles. They feel that by working with weights in a gym they can improve as runners more than if they just go running. This is so if they have time to do weight training and the basic running training. If time is always a problem, however, then the running has to come first. Hill running is a very good form of strength training, and one that we can all do. Just running up hills strengthens the leg muscles so it can be useful to include hills in your regular running route. Some runners actually build a training session around a hill, sprinting up and jogging down several times. This is also a form of repetition training, described in more detail below.

REPETITION RUNNING AND INTERVAL TRAINING

REPETITION RUNNING AND INTERVAL TRAINING are terms used by athletes and coaches to describe particular types of speed training sessions. They are usually, but not necessarily, done on a running track and often timed by a stopwatch.

INTERVAL RUNNING consists of running fast several times over a short distance, 100 to 400m depending on the event being trained for. Between each run is a recovery period of slow jogging or walking. A typical interval session might be to run 100m in 18 seconds, jog back to the start, repeat the run, jog back and so on, ten times.

REPETITION RUNNING is similar except that the recovery is more complete, allowing the running to be faster. For instance, you could run 100m in 15 seconds, ten times, with a 2-minute recovery between each run. Repetitions and intervals can be run over distances as short as 30m for sprinters, or a mile or more for marathon runners.

FARTLECK The Swedish word 'fart' means 'speed', so there! Fartlek means 'speed play' and is a type of training that combines some of the elements of interval training with those of long runs. Typically it is done over parkland or woods, but can be done over any kind of terrain. It is good to include a few hills. Fartlek consists of running – at varying speeds – bursts of faster running with periods of slower running to allow the body to recover. As it is difficult to explain, and to understand if you are new to running, I'll describe the sort of session I might do.

From home I jog for about half a mile (800m) down a gentle slope in a large park near our house. This warms me up. Then I run hard for about 100m along a path that slopes gently uphill, and jog slowly for about 50m then speed up to a steady pace for another 100m or so. Next I sprint hard up a short slope and down the other side, another 100m, and slow down to an easy jog for 200 to 300m or so. Next I run hard along a muddy track for about 400m. It is slightly uphill and can be very slippery. I sometimes slip over and get back with a muddy backside: good training for balance! I then get out onto the road and have a gentle jog downhill for about 500m, go uphill hard for about 150m and then jog across some playing fields. I do a fast downhill stretch, a jog, some alternate fast and slow sections, then make my way home again. Total distance is about 7.5km, made up of a number of fast runs, hard sprints and slow jogging. It is hard but it is also enjoyable, especially if you do it with someone else; you can make little races out of the fast bits. I sometimes do it with my son, and it used to be great fun, but now he is bigger and stronger than I am, and he outruns me!

TIME TRIALS   are a good way of checking your fitness level, and to prepare for a race. Essentially, a time trial is a run over a specific distance that you time to find out how fast you are. You have already done time trials when you first started running, when you went out to see how far you could run in 10 minutes. Later on you were able to measure the improvement when you found that in the same time you could get a bit further.

If you are preparing for a 10-mile race, for instance, you could run a 5-mile time trial to check your readiness. Work out a 5-mile course, run it a few times to get to know it, and then, a week or so before the race, time yourself, running the course as fast as possible. You can then imagine the race and the kind of speed you may be able to achieve. You might even surprise yourself by doing even better in the actual race because you will not be on your own; other runners will keep you going, and the extra adrenalin will 'get you going' as well. Of course, a race is the best form of time trial there is, but don't expect great things if you have been training hard right up to the race. Ease down on your training for a few days at least, so your body gets to the start line rested and ready to go.

RACING   is the best form of speed training a runner can do. There is a wide range of events today, and they are listed below (see pages 101-4). You will have to experiment with different races many times to find out what suits you best.

For the novice runner, the best advice is to try not to get carried away too fast at the start; you will use up all your energy and will have to struggle to finish; instead try to keep the rest of the field in sight, and save your energy for a sprint finish if you can manage it! The more races you do, the easier it will be to judge the right pace to start off at.

In longer races it is better to start too slowly than to start off too fast. Start too fast and you will soon be forced to slow down. Start too slowly, and you can speed up as you go along, and probably overtake those who started too quickly as they slow down, which is very good for your morale!

When you arrive at the race course, find out exactly where the start and finish are. When you are in your running kit and track suit, you can jog to those points if possible as part of your warm-up. During the race you will then know exactly where you are for the important first and final parts of the race.

As a general rule, make sure you are properly prepared for whichever event you choose. Run the required distance in training (except for the marathon), run within your capacity during the race, and don't flop down like a rag doll at the finish. At the end of the race, walk or jog around while your body is recovering and your heartbeat returns to normal. You will feel rested sooner than if you just collapse.

Each race, and each training session, will teach you a little bit more about yourself. It is worth discussing your training and racing with other runners, especially women, but the important thing is that nobody else can experience your running for you. You can learn a lot from others, so listen to what they have to say. But you will learn more about yourself from yourself, so listen to the messages that your body has for you.

Types of races

SPRINTS: races on the track up to and including 400m are classed as sprints. The starter's commands are 'On your marks', at which you walk up to the start line and get down into the 'crouch' sprint start position (or put your toe just behind the line if you prefer to do a 'standing start'); 'Set' at which you raise your hips and shift your weight forward onto your fingertips (or lean forward slightly for a standing start). You must then be perfectly still until the 'BANG' from the gun that starts the race. You must stay in your own lane marked on the track for the whole race. The main requirements for a sprinter are speed and strength.

MIDDLE DISTANCE: track races from 800m to 5,000m are usually referred to as middle distance, with the 10,000m being long distance, and the 800m now sometimes being thought of as a long sprint.

800m consists of 2 laps of the standard athletic track, starting on a curved line by the finish line;

1500m consists of 3¾ laps of the track starting at the beginning of the back straight;

3,000m consists of 7½ laps of the track, starting at the 200m start, half-way round the track;

5,000m consists of 12½ laps, starting at the 200m start;

10,000m consists of 25 laps, starting by the finish line.

'Standing starts' are always used for these races (not the 'crouch' sprint start). The starter's commands are 'On your marks', when you walk forward from the assembly line to the start line, and stand with your toe behind the line; and 'BANG' as the gun starts the race. The main requirements for the middle-distance runner are speed, strength and stamina; for the long-distance runner stamina is probably the chief requirement.

FUN RUNS are usually runs on the road held over an approximately measured course ranging from, say, a mile to a marathon. The run is not considered to be a race because it is not under Amateur Athletics Association (AAA) or Women's Amateur Athletics Association (WAAA) rules. This means that a person of any age can run unless stated on the entry form. Fun runs have become extremely popular in the last few years, and because of their less formal approach, have attracted many women into running.

ROAD RACES: road races are held on roads and footpaths, usually over distances ranging from 5 miles to marathon and more, sometimes combined with shorter races for young age groups. Ten miles (16km) is a very popular distance, and is a much easier target to aim for than a marathon. All road races have a large element of fun running about them, and they are advertised in the athletics and running magazines. Remember that if you join an Amateur Athletic Association (AAA) affiliated club, you will get reduced entry fees for races, as well as the social advantages of having a club to run with. In 1984 there was a series of women-only road races; Avon Cosmetics also sponsor a number of women-only events.

MARATHON: the marathon is 26 miles 385 yards (42.195km) and is a long, long way to run. To do a marathon you need to have done a great deal of running – many, many miles for at least six months or a year. If you are not properly prepared, you risk injury. However, marathons such as the London, New York, Melbourne and other well-publicised marathons have brought many women into running, and it is possible to make a marathon your first race. Claudia, for instance, ran a marathon only one month after she started running. Wet sponges and drinks are usually provided at 5km intervals, but it takes practice to take a drink without stopping. Do not take alcohol during a marathon, it can be fatal. The last few years have also seen the introduction of a number of half-marathons (13.1 miles). These races are becoming extremely popular. In the United Kingdom, the first women's marathon was held at Feltham in 1976.

CROSS-COUNTRY:

in the winter large numbers of runners take part in the British Area Cross-Country League races. There are separate races for women, and for the younger age groups. Distances are almost always shorter than road races, usually 5,000m or less for women. As well as the League cross-country races, there are open cross-country races that anyone can enter. These are usually advertised in athletics and running magazines. There are also some longer cross-country races that you may see advertised such as the 80-mile South Downs Way race.

ORIENTEERING

began in Scandinavia and combines walking or running in the countryside with map-reading. At most events there are several courses of different lengths to suit all competitors, from novice to expert. Competitors start at timed intervals, and use a map to find their way around a series of checkpoints. The competitor who visits them all in the shortest time is the winner. As you can find yourself running through thick undergrowth a full track suit helps to protect you; in fact rules require that competitors must have full body cover to prevent the transmission of diseases caused by possible infected scratches. You will also need a whistle – six blasts repeated at minute intervals if you should need help for any reason. You also need a pen to copy the course from an original map onto your competitor's map, and a polythene bag to protect your map from rain.

FELL RUNNING

originated in Britain and is best known in Scotland, the North of England, Wales, Ireland and the Isle of Man. It involves running up the side of a mountain, or hill and down again. Similar events are held in the United States.

VETERAN RACES:

women over thirty-five and men over forty are classified as veterans – the age difference is, apparently, to keep women in sport. 'Veteran' athletes are divided into various age groups: thirty-five to thirty-nine, forty to forty-four, forty-five to forty-nine, fifty to fifty-four and so on. Various national and international events are held; for instance the 1984 European Championship which was held in Brighton, England. In June 1985 World Championships will be held in Rome, Italy. Events range from 100m sprints to the marathon. Again, you don't necessarily have to be 'good' to compete but it is worth remembering that national events are cheaper to enter; participation in international events can be quite expensive.

Equipment

For racing you need vest, shorts and training shoes. For track races spiked shoes ('spikes') are best, with 6mm spikes for synthetic tracks and 9mm spikes for cinder tracks. You will also need spikes for cross-country races, perhaps with 12mm spikes to get a grip if the course is very muddy. Alternatively, a pair of trainers with a studded or 'waffle' sole will grip slippery surfaces. You will also need a track suit or other warm clothing, and trainers to do your warming up, jogging and to put on after the race. Road racers will need light shoes, with comfort more important than weight for a marathon. Vaseline is useful for putting on toes, heels, insides of thighs, or anywhere where clothing or skin might rub and cause chaffing. A polythene bag is handy for your track suit while you are actually running the race, and a towel and change of clothing for your comfort after the race. And, of course, you will also need waterproof clothing for when it rains.

The need for care

Once you have become addicted to running, the worst thing is to be laid off by an injury that could have been avoided. Injured runners are very bad tempered!

Running is a natural form of exercise but because we, as women, have been prevented, or have prevented ourselves, from doing any exercise in the form of running, we may have weaknesses; for instance, in our feet, legs or back that we didn't know we had before we started. It is not just weakness that causes injury; other causes include doing too much or sudden over-training. Always build up running time and mileage slowly. Starting new exercise means you are working muscles that may not have been used vigorously in that way before, so they often ache. If you have continuous pain when you run, this is an injury and a visit to your doctor is important.

THE VISIT Warning: Many doctors do not understand runners and can be unsympathetic. Some may be helpful but others may tell you to stop running; they are unlikely to tell you what is wrong, nor how best your injury should be treated. Such doctors can be very patronising, saying either that you are too young, or in my case, too old for 'this sort of thing'. So, before you visit a doctor, look up your injury in a sport's injury book so that you know what you are talking about. If necessary, ask to see a specialist. Women, in particular, are often patronised and humiliated by doctors, so really assert yourself. You pay a lot for medical treatment nowadays and the advantages for health of running more than outweigh the injuries. Don't think either that your running injury is self-inflicted and therefore not worth troubling a doctor with. Think of the numerous smokers, for instance, who use medical facilities everyday to treat their bronchitis. Running is one of the most positive steps you can take towards ensuring your own health, and, if something does go wrong, you have every right to see your doctor and to expect sympathetic treatment.

You might, however, prefer to go to a sports clinic of which there are many around today. Your local running or athletics club should have details and addresses.

Prevention is better than cure

Obviously there are certain precautions you can take to prevent injury. Running style is important. You should run in a relaxed, easy fashion, arms low, body moving loosely and smoothly (see page 71). Don't run on your toes, but try to land heel first so that you are running almost flat-footed. In this way you will avoid putting too much strain on your leg and other muscles.

Watch out for holes in the road, uneven surfaces, glass, railings, cars and all other obvious and not so obvious dangers. I had very weak ankles when I started running and used to turn them very easily; as a result I had to take particular care and watch where I was running. If your ankles are weak, however, it often helps to exercise them (see page 106).

Make sure your running shoes are in good condition as well. Worn soles frequently create injuries as they provide no protection from continual contact with the ground.

Warming up and warming down

Before you do any vigorous running, you should spend some time 'warming up'. You don't have to spend long – say 5 to 15 minutes depending on how much time you have available – but it is essential. Warming up prepares your cardiovascular system and your muscles for vigorous activity, and helps to prevent not only stiffness but also injury. For this reason you should get into the habit of warming up very early on. A typical warm up session consists first of mobilising and then of stretching exercises, or of jogging or walking if you are new to running, and should be done before any run let alone before training or racing.

By contrast, 'warming down' comes at the very end of your running or training programme. Essentially it gives your body a chance to 'cool off', to return to normal after vigorous exercise. You should never stop running abruptly; instead walk around or jog slowly for a few minutes until your pulse rate has returned to normal.

Before any track training or racing it is essential to do a 10-minute warm-up of mobilising and stretching exercises, and some jogging. In addition, before short-distance races, you should do about five 50m strides, that is fast, relaxed running. Run 50 metres fast and relaxed with the wind behind you (to make it easy), walk back and do it again five times. This will bring your pulse rate up ready for a fast run.

Mobilising exercises

These loosen up the joints and in a warm-up session should be done before stretching exercises. Start with the head. Keeping your body still, roll your head round in a circular action, first to the right, then to the left. Repeat three times. Next your shoulders. Again, keep your body still. Shrugging your shoulders up, roll them back and forwards in a circular motion. Repeat three times. Follow this exercise with arm circling. You can either circle both arms together, or one at a time. Keeping your arms straight, stretch your arm out to the front, up, back and round to the front again in a large, circular movement. Repeat three times. Mobilise the waist next. Stand, legs slightly apart. Keeping your upper body straight, push your waist round in a circle three times. To mobilise your ankles, sit on the floor, legs stretched out in front of you. Keeping your feet straight, move them down and then up again. Repeat three times. Still with your legs in front of you, move your feet first to one side, then to the other. Again do this three times.

Stretching exercises

For me yoga is the best form of stretching exercise, and I also find the slow inhalation and exhalation of breath very relaxing. Even so, there are some specific stretching exercises that can usefully be done. Hold each position for 5 to 20 seconds, and then repeat each exercise three times.

1 HAMSTRING STRETCH: this stretches the hamstring, a group of three muscles at the back of your leg, from the buttock to the back of the knee. It is done with a table or something of equivalent height. Stand with your left foot on the floor, the right on the table. Lean gently forward, and hold or touch the toes of your right foot. Hold position, then change feet.

2 CALF STRETCH: this stretches the calf muscles, and the achilles tendon attaching the calf muscles to the heel bone. Stand facing a wall, about 90cm from it. Lean forwards so that your forearms are resting flat on the wall, legs straight, feet together, heels on the ground. Gently press your hips forward. You should feel a slight stretch on the lower part of your leg around the calf muscle.

3 QUADRICEPS STRETCH: this stretches the quadriceps, the group of muscles in front of the thigh. Stand on one leg, one arm stretched out for balance. Bring the other leg up behind you, knee bent. Grasp your ankle and pull your leg back. You should feel the pull on the front of the thigh. Change legs and repeat.

4 HIP FLEXORS: this exercise stretches hips, calves and quadriceps. Stretch one leg out behind you, keeping the knee straight. Bend the other knee forward. Hold position. Change legs, and repeat.

5 ADDUCTORS STRETCH: this stretches the adductors, the muscles inside the thigh. Bend one leg at the knee; stretch the other leg out to the side. Hold this position. Change legs and repeat the exercise. You should feel a pull inside the thigh near the groin.

Injuries

When I have suffered injury it is usually because I have overdone it. My first injury, for instance, was to my back and was caused by overdoing weight training, following a schedule that was too hard for me and supervised by an inexperienced person. My second injury was a very painful foot condition called Plantar Fasciitis, an

Stretching exercises

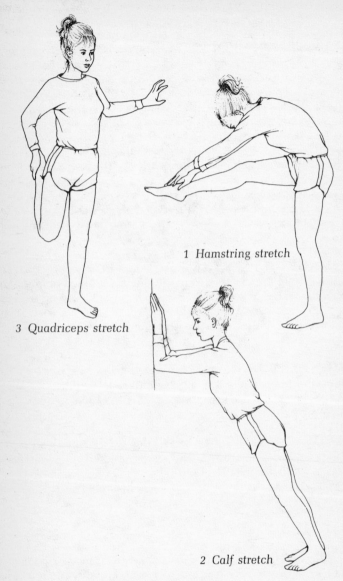

1 Hamstring stretch

3 Quadriceps stretch

2 Calf stretch

4 Hip flexors

5 Adductors stretch

Figure 9.2 Stretching exercises

inflammation of ligaments in the sole of the foot. That too was caused by my doing too much, by suddenly doing a lot of speedwork – track training and short races – when I had only previously done steady distance work. It forced me to stop running for three months while it cleared up and even then it recurred at a later date. Physiotherapy, exercise and a long rest ultimately helped.

These are only two examples. And they could have been avoided. Paradoxically, the fitter you are through running, the more likely you are to become injured because you are more likely to train to your body's limits, and maybe to push yourself to the point where something breaks down. With care and attention, you will, hopefully, avoid serious injury. By and large, it is true to say that injuries are most likely to happen to people who run 30 or more miles a week. Even so, I think it is worth describing some of the most common injuries suffered by runners.

SHIN SPLINTS: this is soreness on the outside of the shin bone, or to the side of the bone. It can be caused by doing too much too soon, and especially by running on hard surfaces. As the calf muscles become stronger, those at the front of the leg become weaker by comparison; in effect, muscle development is unbalanced. To avoid shin splints, build up your running gradually, avoid hard surfaces, and always warm up before running. If it occurs, put ice packs on the soreness, and ease up on your running temporarily.

STRESS FRACTURE: this usually occurs in the bones of the foot or lower leg. It is a break, barely visible on an X-ray, that is caused by excessive mileage and pounding on hard surfaces. It needs a number of weeks of complete rest to mend. Swimming and cycling are alternative exercises that will keep your heart and lungs in good condition while you are not running. When you start running again, begin gradually and build up slowly; make sure your shoes are in good condition.

ACHILLES TENDONITIS: tendonitis is inflammation or swelling of a tendon, in this case the achilles. It is painful and tender when touched. If the condition is not too bad, it is possible to continue running so long as you cut down distance, run on flat ground, and do gentle calf-stretching exercises before you run. High-heeled shoes cause the tendon to shorten, so if you have always worn high heels, make sure you do calf-stretching exercises before you run.

HEEL BRUISE: this is a bruise on the base of the heel, below the skin. It is not visible but hurts every time the heel hits the ground. It is caused by pounding of the heel, and can be prevented by wearing shoes with good heel padding. If it occurs, it can be treated by physiotherapy; meanwhile you can continue running but should use padded heel inserts. You should also run on grass where possible.

KNEE PROBLEMS: the knee is a joint where ligaments, tendons, muscles and bones are secured, and it takes a lot of punishment from runners. Awkward running styles, or over-use can put extra strain on knees. If you get knee pains that do not go away overnight, see a doctor, physiotherapist, or other sport's injury specialist.

BLISTERS: some runners are lucky and never get blisters, others seem to get them all the time. Some runners advise running in two pairs of thin socks to prevent blisters, others say wear no socks at all. My favourite remedy is to prick the blister with a sterile needle (held in a flame to sterilise it). I then put antiseptic on it, and cover it with a plaster. I find that I can then run on it. If you find running too painful, stop. Otherwise you will run awkwardly trying to favour the affected foot, and may cause strain elsewhere.

HEAT STROKE: this is a great danger, and it can kill. Essentially heat stroke is caused through dehydration, when the body's fluids have been depleted. And it occurs when runners have not taken enough fluid before, or during, a race. Heat stroke does not only happen in marathons, but also in 10km fun runs as Val found out. Symptoms of heat stroke are cessation of sweating, headache, a feeling of dizziness and confusion, and weakness. Stop running immediately if you get these symptoms. Drink water or an electrolyte drink which replaces essential salts and minerals, and rest in a cool place. These measures are usually completely effective.

Always listen to your body – do not overdo running. It is good and enjoyable and it is very easy to become a compulsive runner. This might sound strange to the new runner, but runners often feel bad if they haven't been out running. If you are injured and cannot run, and need the exercise to keep your body feeling well, have a swim instead. Swimming is relaxing and keeps the weight off your legs so that they will get better sooner. Alternatively, or as well, you can do a few gentle exercises.

Training schedules

Most top runners, and those who like to race and perform well, keep to a hard training schedule. Some examples follow. To race at high level means training twice a day, and most runners have home, work or other commitments as well. Top women train just as hard as top men but never get the recognition that they deserve.

CHRIS BENNING   Chris Benning is a UK middle-distance runner who races at world-class level. Perhaps unusually for a top-class runner she is very aware of how important it is to encourage joggers, and women in particular. She works as a part-time lecturer at Eastleigh College of Further Education, has run women's jogging groups and, in 1984, organised the first UK Women's Day of Running seminar which was a very stimulating and successful day.

The schedule below covers one week of Chris's winter training schedule. Most of Chris's runs were at 6-minute mile pace, although the runs on the Wednesday evening were often faster. During this week, Chris carried out a particularly high mileage; normally her weekly mileage varies between 50 and 70 miles.

January 1984

Sunday 15	12 miles around Hamble Country Park on trails 40 mins mobility sessions
Monday 16	Weights session and 7-mile run (42 mins) 4½ miles at work
Tuesday 17	Fartleck on grass for 1 hour 4½ miles at work
Wednesday 18	4½ miles at work 7 miles hard
Thursday 19	Steady run on grass trails for 1 hour 5 mins
Friday 20	8 miles including 6 × 6 secs fast stride Weights session and 4 miles steady

Saturday 21   Crystal Palace under the observation of coach, Harry Wilson, 6 × 1,000 hilly circuits with 30 secs recovery. After, mini-circuit training including strides, sit-ups, press-ups, squat thrusts

Chris ran in the 1984 Los Angeles Olympics despite an operation on her leg in 1983 and further illness, much of it due to the tremendous stress put on British middle-distance women runners as a result of the sudden acceptance of the white South African runner, Zola Budd. Chris, like many other British women runners, suffered continual harassment from the press about the situation. Despite these pressures, Chris did make the Olympics, and this is her build-up to her 1500m final. Her schedule is very much in diary form and includes comments about her runs, and how she felt, something that I do myself, and recommend to other women runners:

Summer 1984
July
Monday 30   Went for steady run along coastal roads around San Diego. Very hot, hilly and kerbstones were too high. Legs felt OK. Have recovered from cramp which prevented me from training yesterday (cramp probably due to long flight and the doctor advised me not to train). Strides on track 2 × 60m, 80m, 150m and 3 strides from starts around bend. Still felt sluggish from jet lag.

Tuesday 31   Went in hired car to Mission Bay Park to find some grass. Ran for 35 minutes at steady pace. Very hot again. Track session 4 × 3 × 200m with 4 minutes between sets and 30 secs between reps. in 29.2, 29.6, 28.9/28.7, 29.5, 29.4/28.7, 29.7, 28.5/27.9, 29.3, 28.6. Felt very good and Harry (coach) was very pleased.

August
Wednesday 1   50-min. run around Balboa Park with Martin (we hired a car to get out to the city parks).
Speed session on grass – sprint drills, and 6 × 100m. Legs felt heavy.

Thursday 2   Steady run for 20 minutes around Mission Bay Park.
Mobility exercises and short jog.

Friday 3   Ran 3 × 500m with Martin aiming for 80 secs – 79.5, 80.2, 78.2 with 7 mins recovery. Felt good.
Steady 25 mins run with Gill Hackey around Mission Bay Park.

Saturday 4   Very slow jog for 55 minutes around Mission Bay Park.
Mobility session; travelled to Los Angeles.

Sunday 5   Track session at UCLA 6 × 200m first two steady (30.0, 29.5), second two change of pace 60m steady – 70 fast – 60m steady (28.5, 28.7) and last two 60m fast – 70m steady – 60m fast (27.9, 28.00).
Pleasing times. Lovely track.

Monday 6   Steady 40-min run.
Two miles fast and mobility exercises.

Tuesday 7   First round of 1500m cancelled so short track session similar to Sunday. 4 × 300m at varying pace.
Jogged 3 laps of field (2½ miles).

Wednesday 8   Rest and mobility session.
Jogged 2 laps of field.

Thursday 9	Short jog and mobility exercises. Heat of Olympic Games 1500m – 1st equal in 4:10.2. Had difficulty recovering afterwards due to smog affecting my breathing and had a tension headache. Felt increasingly relieved to have qualified for final.
Friday 10	Exercises plus 40-min slow jog.
Saturday 11	Rested as much as possible (Harry's advice was to spend as much time as possible horizontal!) Ran in 1500m final. 5th in 4:04.7.

CAROLINE RODGERS

Caroline Rodgers is a long distance runner and great advocate of these events for women. During the 1970s she entered a number of men-only 10-mile races unofficially as C. Rodgers. Despite being warned that she could be banned from racing, she went on to run. In fact it is very much thanks to runners such as Caroline that women now have the opportunity to participate in these events; it hasn't always been as easy as it is today.

Like so many top-class runners, Caroline was reaching peak fitness as a marathon runner with a personal best (p.b.) of 2 hours 44 minutes 17 seconds when injury struck. Fortunately she has now recovered and has recently returned to the racing scene. Her marathon schedule is as follows:

Monday	10 miles easy 70 minutes ½-hour swim; 1 hour weights 6 miles fast run
Tuesday	Track session 8 × 400
Wednesday	10 miles easy 10 miles fast plus hill repetitions e.g. 10 × 150m hills

Thursday	Fast 15 miles 1 hour 35 minutes
Friday	Half an hour swim
Saturday	10-mile fartleck
Sunday	Steady run: 20 miles (2 hrs 20 mins)

Before a race, Caroline cuts down her mileage to 30 miles for that week. She also stops weight training.

CAROLINE HORNE   Caroline Horne (Simpson) has had her fair share of setbacks. She also has never had the 'natural' speed that some athletes are fortunate enough to have. Even so, Caroline has tremendous stamina, strength and determination. Her personal best for 10 miles stood, in 1984, at 56 minutes 15 seconds.

A typical week's schedule for Caroline looks like this:

Sunday	12-14 miles; 6 – 6:15-min. per mile pace
Monday	5-mile easy 5-mile fartleck including warm up
Tuesday	8-mile fairly hard
Wednesday	4 miles 2½ mile warm-up; 6 miles including hills; 10 × 200m hill
Thursday	5 miles steady 4 miles steady
Friday	(assuming there is no race the next day) 4 miles 1½-mile warm-up; 2 × 1½ mile fast with ½ mile recovery between each 1½ mile; warm down

Saturday   8 miles steady (assuming there is no race the next day)

Before an important race, Caroline drops her mileage down to 40 to 50 miles per week. For less important, shorter races such as league cross-country races she will probably have a shorter run in the morning before racing in the afternoon.

10 WOMEN HELPING WOMEN

A first for women: the Hastings Women's Day of Sport

It was a warm, sunny autumn day in 1981. I was running round the park with a new-found friend Eileen. She had only recently begun to run, following a suggestion made by my husband Bob that she jog while her daughter, a keen high jumper, trained. Eileen did just that – it gave her a reason to be at the track with her daughter, and also it was something for herself. Gradually she ventured out more, and we began to jog together regularly in the park. That autumn day, as we were running, Eileen suddenly said 'You know Liz, I don't want to go home and do the washing up, I just want to run'. I knew exactly what she meant. Not that I do a lot of housework but even that little became irrelevant once I took up running.

After Eileen's comment I began to think very seriously about women and running, and women and sport in general. I think that sport is one of the most liberating experiences of all for women. It's hardly surprising that it's been kept from us because if we find something, like running, that we can do outside the house, that gives us freedom and makes us feel good, then things like housework are going to become very much less important. Thinking about Eileen, myself and other women, I realised that most women don't know that they can run; it's not an automatic assumption that we make. If we do start, it is either because someone in the family already runs, or because someone has suggested it. And that doesn't just apply to running, there are a lot of other sports that women might be interested in but are often too frightened to try or are completely unaware of. I asked myself: how are women going to participate in sport unless there is someone there to show and encourage them? It is not enough to say 'go to a sports centre'; sport in general is a male domain and sports centres can be very intimidating places. At this point ideas started whizzing around my head – what was needed was a women's day of sport, a day set aside for women only, when they could try out a number of events with a coach present to give advice and encouragement and when, because of the absence of men, no woman would have to feel intimidated.

Not long afterwards I went to our local sports centre and approached one of the supervisors, Bob, with my idea. He thought it was good and suggested that I spoke to Shiona, the other supervisor. Shiona was very enthusiastic, the manager agreed and was also enthusiastic, and Shiona and I set to work. Our first task was to find sponsors so that the day itself could be presented as cheaply as possible, most women having very little money. I wrote to various companies, including sports companies, for sponsorship and in each letter listed my three aims which were:

1 **To encourage women to take an active part in sport, and to realise the enjoyment they can achieve.**
2 **To break the barriers and attitudes towards women in sport, and to how women see themselves.**
3 **To make women aware of the opportunities for them in sport.**

We received nothing from these companies. In January 1982 I wrote to the London and South-East Region Sports Council asking them for a grant. 1982 was their Year of Women in Sport and yet, amazingly, they had made no plans for a women-only event. As a result, ours was to be the first of its kind in the United Kingdom – a very exciting prospect. The Sports Council sent us a grant form and we chose a time and date – 9.30 to 4.30, 12 June 1982.

From this point things really started to move. We decided that there should be as wide a range of sports available as possible and that the day's activities should include running, popmobility, weight training, badminton, squash, netball and volleyball. Two other extra activities would be offered in the afternoon, namely trampolining and table tennis. In addition there were to be films and discussions on the subject of women and sport. The price for the day was set at £2.50 per person to cover four chosen activities, plus the two extra activities and use of swimming pool throughout the day. I drew up twelve different groups of options – A to L. – each group being made up of four activities. Anyone choosing Group A, for instance, would do running, badminton, popmobility and weight training, while someone choosing group L would do running, popmobility, squash and netball. And so on. We also decided on 40-minute sessions for each activity and, with much head scratching and false starts, arrived at a complete timetable of events.

There were some disappointments, all of which reflected the low status of women in sport. We had hoped that, on the day, the sports centre would be closed to men completely so that women would feel absolutely free and unself-conscious. It was, however, argued that this was not financially viable; in the end we managed to get exclusive use of all the sports centre apart from one squash room and the swimming pool which remained open as usual. Nor were we able to use women coaches only; we had male coaches for volleyball, squash and weight training. The men were, however, completely sympathetic to, and understanding of, the needs of women. Our biggest difficulty was organising a creche, something that is absolutely crucial for many women. The room in the sports centre normally used as a creche was to be used for films and discussions, and finding an alternative proved impossible. I tried to get a play bus but without success so that, when the event was advertised in the local press, I made a special plea for helpful boyfriends, husbands, grandparents and so on.

Finally, my biggest concern was what sort of response we were going to get. Our local newspaper ran a feature headed 'Liz Plans to get Women on the Move', and while the Sports Council continued to run advertisements, we had posters printed and distributed around Hastings. The application forms and choice of activities were kept at the sports centre, and we waited. Slowly but surely the enquiries came in. By Friday June 11, the eve of the day, there had been sixty applicants, their ages ranging from seventeen to sixty years of age.

That evening we decorated the sports hall and entrance with posters and information about women in sport, and then waited for the next day. I don't think I have ever been so nervous.

THE BIG DAY; SATURDAY 12 JUNE   Needless to say on the actual day I arrived at the sports centre early and still nervous. Shiona was there, calm and unruffled, but, despite the sixty applications, I was worried that women might not turn up. And even if women did arrive, I was anxious about how the day was going to turn out, having my own expectations of what should happen and how women would feel. Shiona had always been confident and in the event I need not have worried. Gradually women began to arrive at the sports centre, a total of seventy in the end. And slowly, despite my nervousness, the sports centre began to buzz.

Shiona and I introduced the day and then left it up to others to speak. We had invited Claudia Gould (see page 1) to open the day; she had already been running for some years, and had done some radio programmes on running, and is a joy to listen to. Lynn Fitzgerald, then holder of the women's 50-mile track record, also came. Claudia gave a most interesting and enthusiastic talk, followed by Lynn who spoke about her world record and how she had started to run just a few years previously. The introduction was perfect – relaxed and friendly. It warmed everybody up, and initiated one question after another from the women, very unusual as so many public speakers are greeted by stony silences. Women were laughing and relaxed, and the day had hardly even started. In the general discussion one woman commented how squash had helped her to cope with the ironing. She then turned to me and asked whether running had had the same effect. 'No', I replied, 'nothing gets done in our house, we are all too busy running!'.

After the introduction, the day of events started and continued throughout more smoothly than I could ever have hoped. Most of the women who came had done very little sport, while those who had done some wanted to try out new activities. Interestingly, none of the women there had ever done any running. For me, the high point was definitely introducing women to running, which Claudia, Eileen and myself did by taking groups of women running through the fields behind the sports centre.

The day was an enormous success. All I could see were smiling faces as women genuinely enjoyed themselves talking, participating, sharing and laughing, generating a warm, friendly and supportive atmosphere. There was no competitiveness; instead, women helped and encouraged each other and had fun doing so. Without a creche, some women brought their children who likewise joined in the events quite happily and without fuss. A few men also turned up to watch but were, for once, absolutely outnumbered, and frankly I don't think many of the women even noticed that they were there – a very salutory and unusual experience for most men!

When the day finally finished, Shiona and I flung our arms around each other; we wanted to cry – it had been such a successful and thrilling occasion. For us it had proved something very important – that women do enjoy each other's company, something that men find very threatening. Also that the women had no wish to compete with each other, and that in an all-women environment, nobody cared about appearance or ability. In that atmosphere, women found it easy to open up to each other, and to break down conventional barriers. During breaks for coffee or discussion, women who had never met before were talking on an intimate level about their lives. And, most importantly, women who had probably never done any sport since leaving school had experienced and enjoyed sport on a non-competitive basis without feeling that they had to achieve anyone else's standard or excellence. Finally, too, women found that sports centres need not be intimidating places; all of them took away good memories of the Hastings sports centre. The happy atmosphere and the sadness felt when the day ended certainly proved just how important these events are.

Unfortunately, the *Hastings Observer* did not recognise the importance of the day. The editor confined his report to a small article on the back page, illustrated with a tiny, blurred photograph and under the patronising heading of 'Great for Girls and Grannies', a trivialising approach found only too often in the press, and a particular shame as their female reporter had been very enthusiastic.

This was, however, the only jarring note. Local press apart, the day was an enormous success; even those initially opposed to it, such as the head of the recreation department, wrote to me afterwards with warm congratulations, while the women themselves kept asking when the next women's day would be held. Perhaps the feelings are best summed up by a sixty year old woman who came to the Day and said 'I really enjoyed it. Everybody's been so kind and friendly and helped you in what you wanted to do. I don't do a lot of sport, but when I found I couldn't do something, I just had a rest until the next exercise'.

A number of things made the day so successful. One was certainly mine and Shiona's firm conviction that women can gain immeasurably through sport; another was Shiona's position. It's rare to find a female supervisor in a sports centre, most of them are men. Having Shiona, however, meant that I myself got to know the sports centre better, and that the day and the facilities were organised by women for women, a sure formula for success and something that is very unusual in sport. Finally, of course, the women themselves who came along did more than anyone else to make the day a triumph. For most the day served as a unique introduction to sport set in an environment that was relaxed and that was, because of the absence of large numbers of men, completely unthreatening. Since that day more women have been using the Hastings sports centre, most of the women who participated have continued to maintain their interest in sport and in running in particular, and there have been numerous request to repeat the experience. The Sports Council was so pleased with the response that they went on to offer further grants for similar events, a number of which have been held subsequently in London and the South-East of England. That's fine as far as it goes; but there's room for more. I would like to see far more women as staff and managers of sports centres and the Sports Council, and annual women's days held as a matter of course.

Starting a running club

Starting a running club is an excellent way of motivating yourself and other women to run; it is also a way of attracting new runners, and makes running itself into even more of a social occasion. We started our running club – the Hastings Women Runners – immediately after our Women's Day of Sport. At the end of the Day we had collected a list of names and addresses of women who had enjoyed running and who wanted to continue. We decided on a general meeting and advertised this in the local newspaper. At the meeting we talked about how to set up a club, organised meeting times, and places to run, and even decided to affiliate to the then British Women's Cross-Country Association (now the Women's Cross-Country and Road Running Association) and to the Sussex Amateur Athletics Association. The total cost was £15.

We charge an annual £1 membership fee, although not all the people who run with us actually join the club. We also have a discount arrangement with the local sports shop. We meet once a week on a Sunday morning in the local park. We start the morning with a beginner's mile jog, then those who want go on to run further. We also have regular monthly meetings to organise fun runs, swap ideas, and generally discuss running projects. The club does now include men – the Hastings Runners – because there is a need for a low-key running group for men too, although our main aim is still to attract more women into running.

We keep in regular contact with our local newspaper and it reports what the club is doing. We feel this is very important so that local people know that our club is alive and running. We produce a newsletter and keep in touch with each other by telephone or by running around with information. Naturally we had a party to launch the club and have continued with numerous social events.

Enjoyment through running is one of our main aims. And in fact one of our best races was a pram race in aid of local charity. The object was to enter teams of four, one of whom sat inside a pram which was pushed, at a run, around the local pubs, following a prearranged route and having one drink in each pub. I don't know how we managed it, but our four-woman team won and not only won but beat a local football team. Flabbergasted and furious, one of the men from the team came up to me saying 'No way could you have run round that route and drunk alcohol'. But we had, because we are fit women!

11 WHERE TO NEXT? MOBILISING OURSELVES

We've written a book about running for women, but a book by itself is not going to get women on the move. We have to mobilise ourselves. If you are already a runner, or have started recently, perhaps as a result of reading this book, maybe you think, as we do that women runners get a raw deal, and that some changes are essential.

For a start we think that there urgently needs to be a change in media presentation of sport. Whether we are fun runners or top competitors our performances must not be trivialised or our sexuality made fun of. As athletes we must be taken seriously by television, newspapers and magazines. We should be recognised for our athletic abilities and not described in terms of our appearance. We should be described as athletes or runners, not as girls, mothers, housewives or sex objects. To quote from one of the women who went to the Eastleigh seminar: 'It would be a real development for women's running if we could be granted full adult status in magazines, sports commentaries, and events descriptions – do *not* refer to us as "girls" or "ladies" '. Saying this, however, is not enough; I am sure that if we challenge this treatment and oppose it by writing, telephoning, lobbying all forms of the media until we can't be ignored any longer, then we can force change.

We think there is a crying need for women commentators; the media is male-dominated, and there need to be more women, who understand running, commentating on women's events. Likewise, more women journalists should be writing on women's events, which in themselves should be shown in full rather than as brief glimpses. Again, if we make our presence felt, perhaps by writing our own articles and sending them in to magazines, these changes will occur.

Changes in the presentation and practice of physical education in schools are needed, particularly in Britain. Young British women should receive equal opportunities, encouragement and access to sports facilities. There should be far less emphasis on excellence. Obviously the 'gifted' athlete must be encouraged, but overall the emphasis should be on sport for health and fun, so that every girl, whatever her abilities, can reach her own potential. Those of us who are parents can be agitating for these changes, and it is possible to make changes. Only recently some local parents successfully lobbied one of our local co-educational schools on behalf of their nine year old daughter who was not 'allowed' to join the football team. A few letters later and she is now in the team.

We should have more women coaches too; there are far too few. Teenage women in particular require considerable understanding and encouragement but unless women are encouraged to take up running in the first place, this predicament becomes a 'catch-22'.

The British Sex Discrimination Act should be revised also, perhaps along the lines of the American Title IX, so that in Britain, discrimination against women in sport is no longer upheld by the law. We cannot legislate against attitudes but the law must support our efforts in this area as it does in others.

We should also demand equal opportunities for all women in sport, whether able-bodied, disabled and regardless of race. This means the women in the BSAD must be accepted as athletes in their own right. It also means that specialist facilities such as multigyms are as equally available to us as they are to men, such as the Battersea park multigym which is situated in the men's changing rooms. If need be, we should just take them over!

Men, too, should take more responsibility for childcare which again is something that we can encourage. As women we are entitled to leisure activities and should be able to take them for granted as men do. Facilities such as creches are crucial and should be available at more fun runs and other events. It is a fact of life that many of us are prevented from participating because of children, so account should be taken of this need. I am sure that if men had babies there would be creches everywhere.

Figures show just how successful women-only events have been in encouraging women to run. We should perhaps organise more women's fun runs with the emphasis on participation rather than placings. While mixed races are good and do encourage women to build up speed, attention invariably goes to the fastest man. Women-only races are as important to the elite female athlete as to the fun runner as it is only in these that she receives the attention she deserves. We need to give attention to prizes too, and should demand that women and men receive equal prizes. We should also make sure that, in mixed team races, women's teams actually receive prizes, something that doesn't always happen. We should also insist, as Val does, that our placings in events such as the London Marathon be given separately from the men's.

The cost of races too must be kept minimal. The cost of entry goes up continually and in some cases is now as much as £8, which can be out of the reach of many women.

Most of us need more information about running, written

specifically for women, and presented in as accessible a form as possible. Unfortunately, as we found, studies on women and sport tend to be at a very high academic level which makes them difficult to understand. There are plenty of fitness magazines aimed at women, but it would probably be better to have a sports magazine devoted exclusively to women where women at all levels of ability can discuss their particular sport, training needs, problems and so on. Some sections within athletics and running magazines should also be devoted to women. The British magazine *Running* has already initiated a feature devoted entirely to the woman runner; we should push for more or, ideally, write them ourselves. Also use of language in sports books and journals must become non-sexist – there are ways of getting around the gender pronoun 'he' and the longer it is automatically used, the more the idea of sport as male practice will continue.

A good way of passing on information about women and running is to hold regular 'women and running seminars' similar to the one organised by Chris Benning at Eastleigh in 1984. One woman, asked what she had gained from the Eastleigh seminar, said: 'Encouragement and reassurance that other women have the same problems. Also that achievement can be on many different levels.' As runners we need to be reminded of these things, and there is room for many more such seminars. Men tend to be more assertive which often forces us into silence. To overcome this our seminars should be women-only events so that we can, with confidence, discuss and exchange our own ideas as well as getting advice on health and training.

We should insist also that clubs cater for the female jogger/runner of all ages and abilities. One woman, for instance, found that 'recognised clubs are not keen on offering assistance or training people like myself, i.e. a new-to-running veteran housewife'. I wonder how many women have met this sort of response?

Finally, we think that advertisements for running gear should feature women running for fun, women of different shapes, sizes and age, and athletic women. The stereotyped model image must go.

In fact the British Women's Sports Foundation (BWSF) is taking an initiative and is acting as a pressure group and many of the points I have listed are being taken up by the BWSF who are concerned that 'women from all walks of life and at all sporting levels are encouraged to take part and use the group for information or support in the aim to improve the general quality of life.' What the BWSF is doing is very important and every woman runner – able-bodied, disabled and regardless of race – should make contact with them. Their adress is at the back of the book.

What is important too, and very noticeable, is that we as women are finding time for ourselves and, through running and other sports, are making changes to our lives. There already is a British woman's newsletter called *Outdoor Woman* (address at the back of the book) with information on various sports for, and produced by, women. In Britain, however, many of the innovations in women's sport are based in London or other large towns. But not all of us live in the city and it is important that those of us outside should make our voices heard as well. If you live outside a city, you may wish to start a newsletter along the same lines as *Outdoor Woman* but aimed exclusively at women runners, or you may wish to keep a list of running clubs interested in promoting women's running, to start your own group, or to compile a list of women's running events. Your own ideas, views and experiences as runners are invaluable to other women and they should be circulated. We can't leave all the work to organisations such as the BWSF – we need to start our own networks, make contacts with other women runners for ourselves, and to promote our own ideas. And perhaps a network similar to that set up in Canada (see page 44) could be a useful addition to our lives as runners; certainly, it would be a very effective way for woman runners to contact each other. If there are any other ideas I would like to hear about them, or if there are other women interested in starting a woman runner's newsletter or network, please contact our publisher – Pandora Press.

The main thing to remember, however, is that the first step towards mobilising is to start running!

USEFUL ADDRESSES

TRACK AND FIELD ATHLETICS

WOMEN'S AMATEUR ATHLETIC ASSOCIATION (WAAA)

England and Wales WAAA
Francis House,
Francis Street,
London SW1 1DL.

Scottish WAAA
16 Royal Crescent,
Glasgow G3 7SL.

Northern Ireland WAAA
8 Pennington Park,
Cairn Hill Road,
Belfast BT8 46J.

Irish Republic WAAA
Bord Luthleas na Eireann (BLE) Offices,
69 John Road,
Dublin 3.

CROSS-COUNTRY AND ROAD RUNNING

WOMEN'S CROSS COUNTRY AND ROAD RUNNING ASSOCIATION (WCC & RRA)

England
10 Anderton Close,
Bury BL8 2HQ,
Lancashire.

Scotland
114 Canberra Avenue,
Dalmuir West,
Scotland.

Wales
Mr J.H. Collins,
Harriers Haunt,
40 Twyni-Teg,
Killeiy,
Swansea,
West Glamorgan.

Northern Ireland as for the WAAA

Irish Republic as for WAAA

OTHER CONTACTS

Write to the Federation for an up-to-date list of orienteering clubs:
The British Orienteering Federation,
Lea Green,
Matlock,
Derbyshire.

For fell runners write to:
Fell Runners Association,
Membership Secretary N.F. Berry,
165 Penistone Road,
Kirkburton,
Huddersfield HD8 0PH,
Yorkshire.

For Sisters Projects and Running Exchange write to:
57-61 Mortimer Street,
London W1.

For women over thirty-five years:
Women's Veterans' Athletic Club,
15b Mitcham Road,
West Croydon,
Surrey CR0 3JE.
(Secretary Ms Bridget Cushen)

Useful addresses for sport

Sports Council (also a contact for Action Sport and Foundation for Afro Asians in Sport)
16 Upper Woburn Place,
London WC1H 0QP.

British Women's Sports Foundation (to find out what's going on with women in sport)
c/o Sheffield City Polytechnic,
Centre for Geography and Environmental Study,
51 Broomgrove Road,
Sheffield S10.

List of addresses for people with disabilities

British Sports Association for the Disabled,
Hayward House,
Harvey Road,
Aylesbury,
Bucks HP21 8PP.

Northern Ireland Consultive Committee on Sport for the Disabled,
House Of Sport,
Upper Malone Road,
Belfast BT9 5LA.
(Secretary Anne Moorhead)

Welsh Association for the Disabled,
Mrs Roberts,
The Bungalow,
South Wales Equitation Centre,
Heol-y-Cyw,
Bridgend,
Mid Glamorgan.

Scottish Sports Association for the Disabled
W. Fenwick
14 Gorden Court,
Dalcaverhouse,
Dundee.

ORGANISATIONS FOR SPECIFIC DISABILITIES

Amputees | British Amputee Sports Association, c/o British Sports Association for the Disabled, as above.

Blind | British Association for Sporting and Recreational Activities of the Blind, Mr R. Tinsley c/o RNIB, Chaucer Street, Nottingham NG1 5LR.

Scottish Association for Sporting and Recreational Activities of the Blind, Mrs McKay, 43 Helmsdale Avenue, Kirkton, Dundee, Tayside.

Cerebral Palsy | The Spastic Society, 16 Fitzroy Square, London W1.

Deaf | British Deaf Sports Council, R. Haythornthwaite, 38 Victoria Place, Carlisle CA1 1HU.

Mental Handicap | United Kingdom Sports Association for People With Mental Handicap, c/o Sports Council, 16 Upper Woburn Place, London WC1H 0QP.

Paraplegic | British Paraplegic Sports Society, Ludwig Guttmann Sports Centre, Harvey Road, Aylesbury, Bucks HP21 8PP.

(There are English, Northern Ireland, Scottish and Welsh Paraplegic Associations. The above centre will have the addresses.)

Les Autres (The Others)	C. Hodgson, 239A Thomas Close, Southgate, Runcorn, Cheshire.

FURTHER READING

Magazines and periodicals

U.K.

Running
57-61 Mortimer Street,
London W1.

Very informative. Page devoted to women. Good for both serious and fun runner. Gives a diary of races and fun runs.

Athletics Weekly
344 High Street,
Rochester,
Kent.

Weekly magazine. Gives plenty of results and advertises cross crountry, road and track races. More for the serious road, country and track runner.

Marathon & Distance Runner
Peterson House, Northbank,
Berryhill Industrial Estate,
Droitwich, Worcs.

Informative. Gives plenty of results from around the world.

Athletes World
address as for *Marathon & Distance Runner*

Monthly magazine containing results, information, and a section devoted to the veteran athlete.

Outdoor Women
c/o A Women's Place,
Hungerford House,
Victoria Embankment,
London WC2.

Newsletter about activities for women around the country.

AMERICAN PERIODICALS

Runner's World
1400 Stierlin Road,
Mountain View,
CA 94042.

An extremely informative magazine. Prints the most up-to-date information about running and health.

The Runner
P.O. Box 2730,
Boulder,
Colorado 80332.

Very informative. Gives results of races and future events in USA.

Paralysed Veterans of America,
*Paraplegia News/Sports 'n
Spokes*,
5201 N. 19th Avenue,
Suite 111,
Phoenix,
Arizona 85015.

Books

Bayliss, Tony, 'Providing equal opportunities for girls and boys in physical education', report from the ILEA Study Group, Swindon Press Ltd.

Dyer, K.F., *Catching up the Men: Women in Sport* (Junction Books, 1982).

Glover, Bob and Shepherd, Jack, *The Runner's Handbook* (Penguin, 1978).

Hargreaves, Jennifer (ed.), *Sport Culture and Ideology* (Routledge & Kegan Paul, 1982).

Lance, Kathryn, *Running for Health and Beauty* (Proteus Books, 1978).

Lydiard, Arthur with Gilmour, Garth, *Run the Lydiard Way* (Hodder & Stoughton, 1978). (Latest version of this book is called *Running with Lydiard*.)

Porteous, Brian, *Orienteering* (Oxford Illustrated Press, 1978).

Temple, Cliff, *Cross Country and Road Running* (Stanley Paul, 1980).

Twin, Stephanie L., *Out of the Bleachers* (The Feminist Press, 1979).

Ullyot, Joan, *Women's Running* (World Publications, 1976).

Whannel, Gary, *Blowing the Whistle: The Politics of Sport* (Pluto Press, 1983).

INDEX

achilles tendonitis, 110
adductors stretch, 107
aerobic, 89, 98
age and running, 13
Amateur Athletics Union (AAU), 33, 34
anaemia, 58
anaerobic, 98
Andersen-Schliess, Gabriela, 35
androgens, 60
Asian women, discrimination against, 37, 50
asthma, 18-19, 74
Avon International Women's Marathon Championship, 44

Bellotti, Elena Gianini, 48
Bennett, Theresa, 38
Benning, Chris, 112-15
Benoit, Joan, 34-5
bicycle, 28-9
Bingay, Roberta Gibb, 33
Blankers-Koehn, Fanny, 32, 56
blisters, 111
body fat, 61
body temperature, 61-2
bras, 77-8
breasts, 58-9
breast feeding and running, 57
breathing, 72
breathlessness, 83
British National Wheelchair Road Running Committee, 23
British Sports Association for the Disabled (BSAD), 21, 44
British Women's Sports Foundation (BWSF), 43-4, 126

calf stretch, 107
'carbohydrate loading', 88
cardiovascular system, 91
chaffing, 85, 104
childcare, 80
cholesterol, 87
class, and sport, 27-9
clothing, 74-8
comments, 66-7

confidence, 13; lack of, 46-7, 66
Cooper, Dr Kenneth, 89
cross country, 103

de Beauvoir, Simone, 50
de Coubertin, Pierre, 30, 54
diabetes, 19
diet, 87-8
disabilities, 15-24
discrimination, against women in sport, 36-45, 63
dogs, 86
Dublin 10km race, 34
Dyer, Dr Kenneth, 62

endurance events, women's capacity for, 61-2
epilepsy, 15-21
exercise: aerobic, 89, 98; lack of, 10; mobilising, 106; stretching, 106-7

farting, 84
fartleck, 99
fell running, 103
femininity: myths about, 55, 63-4; Victorian cult of, 26-7, 53
Ferris, Dr Elizabeth, 58
fight or flight syndrome, 12
fitness, 8-9; improved, 89-92
Foundation for Afro Asians in Sport (FAAS), 44
Francisco, Eva, 30
fun runs, 94-6, 102

glycogen, 88
Gorman, Mikki, 33
Green, Jimmy, 96

hamstring stretch, 107
Hansen, Jacqueline, 62
Hargreaves, Jennifer, 43
Hartman, Marea, 39-40
Hastings Women Runners, 123
Hastings Women's Day of Sport, 118-22
heart, 89, 91

heat stroke, 111
heel bruise, 111
Heraea, 26
hills: running up, 71, 72; training, 98
hip flexors, 107
'hitting the wall', 88
Horne, Caroline, 116-17

illness, and running, 69
injury, 107, 110-11; prevention of, 104-5
International Amateur Athletic Federation (IAAF), 30, 34
International Olympic Committee (IOC), 30, 32, 36
interval training, 99

jogging, 13, 70; *see also* running

knee problems, 111
Kratochvilova, Jarmila, 40, 41, 50
Kristiansen, Ingrid, 37, 56, 69

London Marathon, 33, 34
loneliness, 11
Lydiard, Arthur, 97

marathon: women's Olympic (1984), 35; first all-women UK, 44-5
marathon running, 102; and pregnancy, 56-7
media, and sexism, 38-41
medical problems, 69
Melopene, 30
menstruation, 57-8
middle distance running, 101
miscarriages and running, 55
muscles, 71, 84-5
myths about women, 27, 30, 55-64

New York City Marathon (1972), 34
New York Mini Marathon, 34
night running, 86
Nike/Women's Own 10km Fun Run (1984), 44
North American Network of Women Runners, 44

Olympic Games: ancient, 25-6; modern, 30; women's events in, 36

orienteering, 103
Outdoor Woman, 126
oxygen, 60-1, 89

patriarchy, 54
Pherenice, 26
pregnancy and running, 56, 69
prizes, 41-2
puberty, 60
pulse rate, 92

quadriceps stretch, 107

races, 94-6, 101-3
racing, 100; equipment for, 104
Radke, Lina, 32
Rand, Mary, 56
Ready, Christine, 45
repetition running, 99
respiratory system, 91
road racing, 102
Rogers, Caroline, 41, 115-16
routine, 85, 92
Rudolph, Wilma, 96
Running, 126
running: and liberation, 13; benefits of, 8-9, 11, 13-14; history of women's, 25-35; improving your, 92-101; myths about, 55-64; recent developments, 33-5; starting, 65-88; techniques of, 71-2, 105; wheelchair, 20-3
'running revolution', 33

safety checks, 69-70
schedule: beginner's, 80-3; training, 112-17
self-consciousness, 50-2, 66-7
Sex Discrimination Act 1975, 37-8
sex testing, 63
sexual harassment, 86
shin splints, 110
shoes, 75-6; spikes, 104
shorts, 77
'Sisters Project', 44
socialisation, 47-50
Sparta, 26
speed training, 98
sponsorship, of women-only events, 44
sport: as 'masculine' activity, 25, 29, 47, 48; at school, 48-9; recent

developments in, 43-5; sexism in, 36-45
Sports Council, 43
sportswomen, media treatment of, 38-41
sprints, 101
stamina, 61-2
stamina training, 97-8
stitch, 83
strength training, 98
stress, 10-12
stress fracture, 110
strides, 106
suppleness, 98
sweating, 74, 84
Switzer, Katherine, 32-3
Szewinska, Irena, 56

testosterone, 60
time trials, 100
Title IX, 37
'Toronto Women Running', 44
track and field events, first women's international, 31

training: need for, 96-7; schedules, 112-17; types of, 97-101
t-shirt, 77

Ullyot, Dr Joan, 69
unfitness, 9-12
urine, leakage of, 83

veteran races, 103

Waitz, Grete, 34
warming down, 106
warming up, 105-6
weather, 73-4
wheelchair running, 20-3
women: attitudes towards, 27; images of, 27, 51; myths about, 27, 55-64; pressures on, 10-12, 50-3; sporting potential of, 59-62; Victorian ideal, 26-7
Women's Amateur Athletic Association (WAAA), 30
Women's World Games, 31

P A N D O R A   P R E S S

an imprint of Routledge and Kegan Paul

For further information about Pandora Press books, please write to the Mailing List Dept at Pandora Press, 14 Leicester Square, London WC2H 7PH or in the USA at 9 Park Street, Boston, Mass. 02108; or in Australia at 464 St Kilda Road, Melbourne, Victoria 3004, Australia.

Some Pandora titles you may enjoy:

WOMEN'S HISTORY IN SHORT STORIES

DARING TO DREAM

Utopian stories by United States women: 1836-1919

Compiled, edited and introduced by Carol Farley Kessler

Carol Farley Kessler has unearthed an extraordinary assortment of visionary writing, writings which encapsulate all the yearnings of a vanished generation for a future which has still to be made. Some women write with irony, describing journeys through time and space to parallel but inverted worlds where sober-suited women run commerce and affairs of state while men either prink and preen in beribboned breeches, or are weakened by the burden of unending housework. Other writers lay out complicated blueprints for a non-sexist society. One woman dreams, touchingly, of a fantastic future where men get up in the night to comfort crying children. The stories demonstrate that even in the early nineteenth century women were arguing that male and female 'character traits' were the product of their roles, not of their biology; and they make apparent the hidden roots of the discontent, longing and anger which was later to erupt in the great movements of women for change.

0-86358-013-0 Fiction/Social History 256pp 198 × 129 mm paperback

MY COUNTRY IS THE WHOLE WORLD

an anthology of women's work on peace and war

Cambridge Women's Peace Collective (eds)

Women's struggle for peace is no recent phenomenon. In this book, the work of women for peace from 600 BC to the present is documented in a unique collection of extracts from songs, poems, diaries, letters, petitions, pictures, photographs and pamphlets through the ages. A book to give as a gift, to read aloud from, to research from, to teach from, *My Country is the Whole World* is both a resource and an inspiration for all who work for peace today.

'An historic document . . . readers will be amazed at the extent of the collection.' *Labour Herald*

'A beautifully presented and illustrated book which makes for accessible and enlightening reading.' *Morning Star*

0-86358-004-1 Social Questions/History 306pp A5 illustrated throughout paperback

DISCOVERING WOMEN'S HISTORY

a practical manual

Deirdre Beddoe

Rainy Sunday afternoons, long winter evenings: why not set yourself a research project, either on your own or in a group or classroom? This is the message from Deirdre Beddoe, an historian who tears away the mystique of her own profession in this step-by-step guide to researching the lives of ordinary women in Britain from 1800 to 1945. *Discovering Women's History* tells you how to get started on the detective trail of history and how to stalk your quarry through attics and art galleries, museums and old newspapers, church archives and the Public Records Office – and how to publish your findings once you have completed your project.

'An invaluable and fascinating guide to the raw material for anyone approaching this unexplored territory.'   *The Sunday Times*

'Thrilling and rewarding and jolly good fun.'   *South Wales Argus*

0-86358-008-4 Hobbies/Social History 232pp 198 × 129 mm illustrated

ALL THE BRAVE PROMISES

Memories of Aircraftwomen 2nd Class 2146391

Mary Lee Settle

Mary Lee Settle was a young American woman living a comfortable life in Washington D.C. when the Second World War broke out. In 1942 she boarded a train, carrying 'a last bottle of champagne and an armful of roses', and left for England to join the WAAF. She witnessed the horror of war – the bombing raids, the planes lost in fog, the children evacuated, a blacked-out Britain of austerity and strain. She also witnessed the women, her fellow recruits, as they struggled to adapt to their new identities and new lives at the bottom of the uniformed pile. Dedicated 'to the wartime other ranks of the Women's Auxiliary Air Force – below the rank of Sergeant', this rare book captures women's wartime experience; a remarkable and important story by one of America's prizewinning novelists.

'One of the most moving accounts of war experience ever encountered' *Library Journal*

0-86358-033-5 General/Autobiography 160pp 198 × 129 mm paperback

not for sale in the U.S.A. or Canada